W9-CKR-167

Strategic Planning
TRAINING

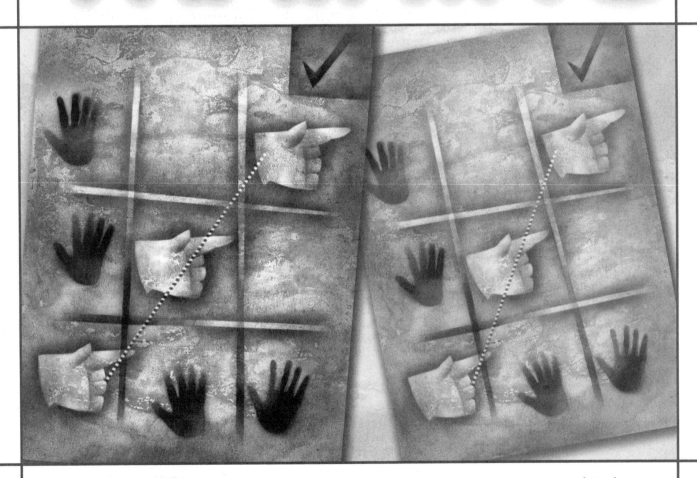

Includes CD-ROM with
Ready-to-Use Microsoft
PowerPoint™ Presentations

Exercises, Handouts, Assessments, and Tools
to Help You:

✔ Create Strategic Planning and Problem Solving
Training at All Levels
✔ Understand Key Concepts, Assess Readiness,
and Avoid Common Pitfalls
✔ Become a More Effective and Efficient Facilitator
✔ Ensure Training Is on Target and Gets Results

Jeffrey Russell
Linda Russell

ASTD Press

ASTD Press is an internationally renowned source of insightful and practical information on workplace learning and performance topics, including training basics, evaluation and return-on-investment (ROI), instructional systems development (ISD), e-learning, leadership, and career development.

Ordering Information: Books published by ASTD Press can be purchased by visiting our website at store.astd.org or by calling 800.628.2783 or 703.683.8100.

Library of Congress Catalog Card Number: 2004116268

ISBN: 978-1-56286-374-6
ISBN: 1-56286-374-6

Acquisitions and Development Editor: Mark Morrow

Copyeditor: Christine Cotting, UpperCase Publication Services, Ltd.

Interior Design and Production: UpperCase Publication Services, Ltd.

Cover Design: Ana Ilieva

Cover Illustration: Todd Davidson

Printed by Victor Graphics, Inc. Baltimore, MD
www.victorgraphics.com

The ASTD Trainer's WorkShop Series is designed to be a practical, hands-on road map to help you quickly develop training in key business areas. Each book in the series offers all the exercises, handouts, assessments, structured experiences, and ready-to-use presentations needed to develop effective training sessions. In addition to easy-to-use icons, each book in the series includes a companion CD-ROM with PowerPoint™ presentations and electronic copies of all supporting material featured in the book.

Other books in the Trainer's WorkShop Series:

- ◆ *New Supervisor Training*
  John E. Jones and Chris W. Chen

- ◆ *Customer Service Training*
  Maxine Kamin

- ◆ *New Employee Orientation Training*
  Karen Lawson

- ◆ *Leading Change Training*
  Jeffrey Russell and Linda Russell

- ◆ *Leadership Training*
  Lou Russell

- ◆ *Coaching Training*
  Chris W. Chen

- ◆ *Project Management Training*
  Bill Shackelford

- ◆ *Innovation Training*
  Ruth Ann Hattori and Joyce Wycoff

- ◆ *Sales Training*
  Jim Mikula

- ◆ *Communication Skills Training*
  Maureen Orey and Jenni Prisk

- ◆ *Diversity Training*
  Cris Wildermuth with Susan Gray

Contents

◆

There are dozens of books on strategic planning and decision making. Why should you buy *this* book? Although we were somewhat hesitant to add another book to the pile, we also felt that this stack of strategic-planning books often created more confusion than clarity in how to do this important work. We felt that there needed to be a book that would serve as both a translator of these diverse texts and a how-to guide for developing the strategic-planning and -thinking and the strategic decision-making competencies of CEOs, managers, supervisors, and frontline employees. This book is our answer to this need.

We wrote this book to help organizational leaders, consultants, and human resource or organization development specialists put their arms around a practical approach for developing and implementing strategy. Our goal was to write a book that provides insight into the strategic-planning and decision-making process and guidance in how to translate these insights into results. We include models, templates, and a flexible set of interactive training modules that you can customize to fit a wide variety of organizations and situations.

The models, methods, tools, and approaches for guiding and facilitating strategic planning and decision making have emerged from our years as consultants to a diverse clientele. Our methods have been tested and found effective in our work with financial institutions, manufacturers, universities, medical institutions, state and local governments, multinational organizations, and even small mom-and-pop businesses.

The CD-ROM accompanying this book offers handouts, tools, training instruments, and PowerPoint slides that are ready for immediate use. With these additional tools, you are encouraged to use the training program designs exactly as outlined in this book or custom-build your own workshops. We believe that this book's greatest strength, however, is that it enables you to build on our models and tools and design the right program to meet your specific needs.

Mark Morrow, the visionary book editor at the American Society for Training & Development, recognized the value of this book as a volume in ASTD's Trainer's WorkShop Series and encouraged us to tackle this subject. His enthusiastic support for the book and his confidence in our ability to write it kept us going. We're glad he kept at it with us.

Because much of the work you see here emerges from our own consulting practice, we have to thank our clients who have helped us learn what works and what doesn't when it comes to strategy formation, strategy implementation, and strategic problem solving and decision making. Their willingness to embrace new approaches to strategic planning allowed us to fine-tune our methods and approaches.

Strategic planning is both an exciting and an exasperating discipline that can lead to astounding results or mediocre outcomes. Whether your strategic-planning efforts lead to one or the other depends on a variety of factors, forces, tools, and methods. We hope that this book moves you and your organization toward the astounding outcomes. If this occurs, we (and, most important, you) have done the right thing.

We'd like to continue our own learning and would greatly benefit from hearing from you—on how you applied the models in this book, what worked, what didn't, and so forth. If you have ideas, suggestions, or questions, or just want to begin a dialogue around strategic thinking and planning, please e-mail us. We look forward to hearing from you.

Good luck in your journey into strategy formation!

Linda and Jeffrey Russell
RCI@RussellConsultingInc.com
Madison, Wisconsin
February 2005

Introduction: How to Use This Book Effectively

What's in This Chapter?

- ◆ Discussion of the value of strategic planning, decision making, and problem solving

- ◆ Explanations of our strategic-planning, decision-making, and problem-solving workshop designs

- ◆ Tips for using this workbook most effectively

- ◆ Enumeration of what's included in this workbook and on the accompanying CD-ROM

When you hear the words *strategic planning* it's likely that a whole host of ideas and images surface for you: being forward thinking, being too top-down, introducing innovation and change, having too much of a focus on control, opening up the organization to new opportunities, having a large gap between what we say we'll do and what we actually accomplish, engaging people's spirits, experiencing analysis paralysis, searching for a way out of the mess, or perhaps just realizing you don't have a clue!

This mix of positive and negative reactions is understandable. Ever since strategic planning emerged as a formal discipline or practice in the 1960s it has had more than its share of proponents and critics. There is much to be said for the discipline. It can certainly help provide direction to organizational efforts. It can be just the right catalyst to get employees moving in the right direction. It can help galvanize efforts of all key stakeholders around a shared vision, which can, in turn, significantly strengthen an organization's ability to be both a great and an enduring organization.

There is, however, much to criticize in strategic planning. It can be ponderously slow. It can focus too much on controlling organizational activity at times when freedom from control is what is most needed. It pretends to predict or foresee a future that is, to quote author and researcher Ralph Stacey, "unknowable." Instead of invention and innovation, strategic planning too often is reduced to an annual or biennial exercise in affirming where the organization has been—not asserting where it needs to be. And too often it is done by the executives and planners in an organization—the people who may be least aware of the rich organizational environment in which most managers and employees work.

The trick to strategic planning, of course, is to find a way to capture all of the positive energy, the potential, the growth and learning, and the nimble responsiveness and organic flexibility that the "good" strategic planning process offers us while avoiding the traps and pitfalls of the "bad" process. Unfortunately, the track record of most strategic planning is rather dismal. Most of the research that exists on the effectiveness of such planning (and there is precious little empirical data out there) has found scant evidence that the process is done well or that, even when done "well," it actually helps organizations deal with the challenges of the market and environment.

This book tries to sort through the complexities of this challenging topic and present to you a simple and direct approach for creating strategy in your organization. Although you and your organization must approach the strategic-planning and decision-making process in your own way (something we'll cover in a later chapter), we think that you'll find our methods and approaches are helpful. At a minimum this book will give you a few more tools in your planning or organizational development tool kit.

The Value of Training to Strategic Planning

There is ample evidence—both anecdotal and empirical—that organizations do a rather poor job of strategic planning and decision making. In a major meta-analytic review of strategic planning research that included 29 empirical studies that sampled 2,496 organizations, B. K. Boyd (1991) found the overall effect of planning on performance very weak.

Despite these results, Boyd remained upbeat about the benefits of strategic planning. He noted that "while the average effect size [in performance] is small, many firms do report significant quantifiable benefits from participating in the strategic planning *process*" [italics added, p. 369]. Regardless of his optimistic tone, his research suggests that, on balance, strategic planning hasn't achieved the results that it set out to accomplish for a company: improved financial performance.

The anecdotal evidence is just as weak. In his seminal work on evaluating the effectiveness of strategic planning, *The Rise and Fall of Strategic Planning,* Henry Mintzberg cited more than 20 years of journal articles written by some of the giants in the field of strategy formation, including Ackoff, Igor Ansoff, and Michael Porter. Mintzberg quoted Ansoff as writing, "in spite of almost twenty years of existence of the strategic planning technology, a majority of firms today engage in the far less threatening and perturbing extrapolative long-range planning" (Mintzberg, 1994).

This book, however, is not about despair in the face of that rather somber assessment of strategic planning's effectiveness. There is a way to strengthen the effectiveness of your methods—one based on the core skill of strategic thinking. By building the competency of strategic thinking into the skill set of all leaders and employees, your organization is more likely to reap the benefits of strategy formulation and implementation.

A skill and knowledge training program, matched with the right strategic-planning framework, culture, and philosophy, can lead to a more meaningful strategic-planning process and one that produces substantive results for the organization's future. In this book we'll help you develop these skills and this knowledge in your staff and offer you a road map for developing the right framework, culture, and philosophy for strategy formulation.

Serving Multiple Organizational Needs

This book strives to address a variety of needs in the organization with respect to strategic planning and decision making. For those new to strategic planning, we offer an overview of the historical foundation of the process, a survey of diverse strategic-planning models, and tips for avoiding the pitfalls and detours that can significantly erode the effectiveness of a strategic-planning process.

For those who already have a good understanding of the process but are looking for a way to develop strategic-thinking and -planning skills in others, we provide a series of half- and full-day interactive workshops that present these skills in an exciting and engaging way. You'll find these customizable workshops great opportunities for engaging employees at all levels of the organization in the process of strategic planning—and that, we believe, is a key ingredient in ensuring the ongoing relevance of the strategic plan.

An added bonus of this book is the inclusion of a powerful tool kit that include a diverse array of methods and techniques to guide problem solving and decision making (PSDM) within a strategic-planning framework. From brainstorming and the nominal group technique to the is/is not diagram and the decision matrix, you'll find this handy tool kit useful as a stand-alone suite of tools that enable any group or team to improve their PSDM skills. We think that you'll find the tool kit helpful regardless of the presence or absence of a strategic plan or a process for developing one.

How to Use This Workbook and Accompanying CD Most Effectively

Whether you are a novice instructor or an experienced trainer, you will find this book a useful resource for designing, developing, and facilitating workshops in strategic planning and PSDM for leaders and staff. By understanding the basic concepts that represent the foundation of strategic planning and decision making and then reviewing the training program designs included in this book, you will be able to custom-design the skill-building training programs you need to present to audiences ranging from your CEO/president to the people who work on the organization's front line everyday.

To benefit most from this book and the accompanying CD, we recommend that you follow these steps as you design your training program:

1. Skim the book. Quickly read through its entire contents. Study the "What's in This Chapter?" list at the front of each chapter. Get a good sense of the layout and structure of what's included in each chapter and in the book overall. Also review the contents of the CD.

2. Become more familiar with strategic planning and strategic thinking. Read chapter 2 for an overview of what strategic planning is and why it's important, and to gain an awareness of the various models and approaches used to guide the process of strategy formulation and implementation. That chapter also lays down the philosophical foundation for planning that must be the backbone of your training program.

3. Assess the organization's readiness for strategic planning and strategic thinking. As you'll learn in chapter 2, such thinking is a way of looking at the world that should be practiced every day by every employee in the organization. Strategic planning, however, calls for an environment that is conducive for planning and strategic management. Chapter 3 introduces some methods, approaches, and tools

for assessing the environment within which strategic planning will need to occur. That chapter will help facilitate the organization's "readiness" to engage in a thoughtful and comprehensive strategic planning process. The key realization from chapter 3 is that strategic planning is likely to be more successful, and hence more effective, when an effort is made to understand the organizational readiness for the process. Although an organization that isn't ready for strategic planning will still need to initiate the process, at least you will begin the effort with an awareness of some of the challenges you are likely to face as you begin. Chapter 3 will also give you targets for some of your skill- and knowledge-building efforts.

4. Review the basics of good program design. Chapter 4 presents an overview of design fundamentals. In that chapter you'll learn how to write good learning objectives and outcomes, identify experiential learning activities that reinforce learning, and explore methods for facilitating participant learning and application. As you'll see, the training programs presented in this book are designed to help bring about learning. In some cases, there will be results or deliverables that can actually be used as part of a strategic-planning process (for example, conducting a SWOT [strengths, weaknesses, opportunities, threats] analysis during the workshop). We believe that you'll find chapter 4 useful, even if you're an experienced trainer. It offers a review of good teaching practices and likely reinforces what you are already doing.

5. Build evaluation into your training program design. Chapter 5 suggests some approaches for measuring learning, behavior change, and results prior to offering your training workshop.

6. Explore the training modules. Chapters 6 through 10 offer a variety of training programs that you can draw on as you design a program to fit both the organization and your audience. These chapters include everything from a half-day program on creating strategic thinkers, to two full-day programs on mastering fundamental and advanced strategic planning skills, to two full-day programs that develop strategic PSDM skills and apply a variety of creative tools.

7. Design your training program. This final step requires you to integrate a better understanding of strategic thinking and planning with an awareness of the organizational climate for strategic planning,

the foundations of good training program design, and the customizable training modules.

All of the tools, training instruments, course handouts, and PowerPoint slides referred to in the modules are included on the accompanying CD-ROM. Because of the breadth and depth of the information contained in this book, the handouts, tools, and training instruments are not reproduced within the text. They are available only on the CD. Follow the instructions in the appendix, "Using the Compact Disc," and the CD document titled "How to Use This CD.doc" to access the various electronic documents.

The training materials in this book and/or on the CD include

- ◆ tools and strategies for assessing the readiness of the organization for strategic planning

- ◆ training workshops that can be used as is or modified in response to the organization, its challenges, and your own teaching style

- ◆ learning activities and supporting training instruments and handouts that are designed to fit into the training modules (chapter 11)

- ◆ tools for facilitating training workshops that encourage active learning, integration of content, and strengthened learning application back on the job (chapter 12)

- ◆ printable documents that can be used as workshop handouts (CD)

- ◆ Microsoft PowerPoint presentations in color and black-and-white for your use in guiding participants' learning and in focusing their energy

- ◆ additional printed and Website resources for future reference in understanding strategic planning and how to design effective training programs.

Icons

For easy reference, icons are included in the margins throughout this workbook to help you quickly locate key elements in training design and instruction. Here are the icons and what they represent:

 CD: Indicates materials included on the CD accompanying this workbook.

Clock: Indicates recommended timeframes for specific activities.

Discussion: Highlights questions you can use to explore important issues as part of a training activity, or times when participants engage in discussion with fellow learners.

Handout: Indicates handouts that you can print or copy and use to support training activities.

Key Point: Alerts you to key points that you should emphasize to participants or that are particularly salient for you as the facilitator.

Learning Activity: Introduces structured or guided experiences to facilitate participant insight, application, and learning.

PowerPoint Slide: Indicates PowerPoint presentations and individual slides.

Tool: Identifies an item that offers information participants will find useful in the training session and on the job, or guidance that the facilitator can use to enhance learning.

Training Instrument: Identifies interactive participant materials that are used before, during, or following the training seminars.

What to Do Next: Highlights recommended actions that you can take to transition from one section of this workbook to the next.

What to Do Next

- ◆ Review the next chapter to better understand the origins of strategic planning and the models that have been developed to define its practice in organizations today.

- ◆ Reflect on your own experience with strategic planning in your current or former organizations. What role did you or HRD play in the process? How effective was the resulting plan? What enabled the plan to be effective—or what caused it to be ineffective?

◆ Begin thinking about where you might start a strategic planning training program for leaders and staff at every level of the organization.

◆ ◆ ◆

The next chapter defines strategic planning, explores its role in enabling organizational success, provides various models for managing the process, and identifies some common pitfalls and challenges that any strategic-planning process is likely to face. The chapter ends with a listing of some resources that we think you'll find useful to deepen your understanding of the complex process of strategy formulation and implementation.

Strategic Planning and Its Role in Organizational Success

What's in This Chapter?

- Definition of strategic planning and its similarities with and differences from strategic thinking

- Description of the role of strategic planning and thinking in long-term organizational success

- Historical perspective on models for strategic planning

What Is Strategic Planning?

The term *strategic planning* is a marriage of two words and two distinct concepts. The first word, *strategy,* is from the Greek *strategos,* which the *Oxford English Dictionary (OED)* defines as "art of the commander-in-chief; the art of projecting and directing the larger military movements and operations of a campaign." The *OED* goes on to suggest that strategy is "usually distinguished from *tactics,* which is the art of handling forces in battle or in the immediate presence of the enemy." So, the first of our terms focuses on *what* to do to fulfill the mission and win the war. Strategy making is therefore a creative process—one that involves imaginative and introspective thought to invent or conceive of a method for achieving the goal. This creative process involves *synthesis*—bringing together creativity, imagination, and intuition to achieve inspired insight about the future direction of the organization.

Planning, on the other hand, is focused on the analytical process of translating strategy into action. The *OED* defines *planning* as "a formulated or organized method according to which something is to be done; a scheme of action, project, design; the way in which it is proposed to carry out some proceeding." Planning, therefore, involves *analysis*—gathering and analyzing information, defining specific operational goals, and then breaking down each of these complex goals into a series of steps and actions.

Taken together, these two words provide insights into the heart of strategic planning and its role in moving any organization into the future: *creating a strategy for achieving the organization's goals and then devising an organized method to accomplish this strategy.*

The Role of Strategic Planning and Strategic Thinking

In his provocative book, *The Rise and Fall of Strategic Planning* (1994), Henry Mintzberg argued that too often strategic planning simply becomes strategic programming that is devoid of imagination and the intuition of strategy formation. In a *Harvard Business Review* article that highlighted the themes from his book, Mintzberg wrote, "Planning cannot generate strategies. But given viable strategies, it can program them; it can make them operational" (p. 112). He also noted that formal planning, "by its very analytical nature, has been and always will be dependent on the preservation and rearrangement of established categories.... But real strategic change requires not merely rearranging the established categories, but inventing new ones" (p. 109).

With Mintzberg's cautionary note in mind, it is important at this point to make the clear distinction between *strategic planning* and *strategic thinking*. Whereas strategic planning seeks to translate strategy into action, strategic thinking seeks instead to understand what is happening in the present and then identify the best response or action in the face of those emerging events. This distinction is important. Although strategic planning offers a formalized plan to realize a desired future, strategic thinking enables the spontaneous discovery and creation of innovative approaches (strategies) that more formal planning could never have imagined.

We believe every organization needs a strategic plan. The value of a plan is in both the discipline it brings by systematically guiding deep reflections about the organization's future and the forces influencing its future and in the resulting road map that charts a path into that future. The formal, step-by-step process of identifying the organization's core purpose or ideology, assessing the complex environment in which it operates, and defining the methods it will use to fulfill this purpose can be a healthy and cathartic exercise that gets the organization to ask the big questions. By itself, however, the strategic plan is not enough. As we suggest in the training modules, developing strategic thinking in organizational stakeholders is just as important as developing a strategic plan. Strategic thinking serves the organization equally well (if not better) by encouraging the consideration and expression of serendipitous insights and contrary thoughts that challenge the status quo represented by and codified in the formal strategic plan.

Strategic thinkers ask the big questions not just at specific planning events, but every day. In posing these questions they serve the organization's long-term future by identifying emerging information, challenges, and opportunities that may have been unknown or absent when the strategic plan was developed. In identifying these emergent issues, strategic thinkers challenge the organization to consider shifting its *deliberate* strategies (the strategic plan). Because no strategic plan can anticipate all likely events—especially during times of tumultuous change—developing strategic thinkers at every organizational level (not just at the top) enables the organization to respond to new information, challenges, and opportunities.

Sustaining long-term organizational success, then, is more than simply having a strategic plan. In fact, the presence of a plan that is not modified and adjusted with good strategic thinking can actually represent a barrier to organizational success. By adhering to a plan that didn't (and couldn't) anticipate emerging events, the organization may miss a key strategic opportunity or fail to respond to a developing threat. When a strategic plan is combined with the competencies of strategic thinking by stakeholders at all levels, the organization is more likely to sustain its success for the long term.

Organizational Longevity

Even with a plan, however, long-term success is far from guaranteed. Citing research conducted by Royal Dutch/Shell, Arie de Geus (1997), the author of *The Living Company*, contended that the average life expectancy of most multinational companies is between 40 and 50 years. He cited evidence that fully one third of the companies listed in the 1970 *Fortune* 500 had vanished by 1983. De Geus is not alone. Ralph Stacey (1992), author of *Managing the Unknowable,* pointed out that five years after Tom Peters and Robert Waterman published their "excellent" companies list, two thirds of the companies had simply disappeared (through mergers, acquisitions, bankruptcies, and so forth).

As we noted in chapter 1 when we cited the work of Henry Mintzberg, there is little evidence that simply having a strategic plan positively influences these rather daunting odds. This evidence of failure, however, should not lead us to the conclusion that strategic planning is beyond redemption. The question is not whether to engage in strategic planning, but how to do it right. Part of this effort involves putting together a thoughtful and inclusive strategic-planning process and part involves developing strategic thinking as a core organizational discipline and competency.

When we do it right and when we develop strategic thinking throughout our organization, we are more likely to develop organizational capacities that promote longevity. De Geus, Stacey, James Collins (*Build to Last,* 1997), and others offer a prescription for long-term success. Their work is woven throughout the models, approaches, and strategies for organizational planning that we present in this book. Although there are no guarantees, there are some actions that you and other organizational leaders can take to move your organization successfully into the future.

Models for Strategic Planning— An Historical Perspective

It is both a challenge and an opportunity of strategic planning that there is no one best way to do it. Although researchers and writers will argue that their proposed process is "the" way to develop a strategic plan, in reality the approach that an organization eventually adopts as its own should be the one that works. The strategic-planning method that your organization embraces should be one that

- ◆ matches (and challenges) your organization's culture and temperament
- ◆ asks the tough questions about fundamental purposes
- ◆ challenges the status quo
- ◆ reflects and responds to the environment within which it operates
- ◆ engages employees at every organizational level
- ◆ is flexible in its approach
- ◆ provides a road map for the organization going forward
- ◆ is continually revised and updated in response to emerging information over the life of the plan.

A full survey of the variety of approaches and methods to strategic planning is beyond the scope of this book, but we think it useful to provide a brief overview of the techniques that are in use today. The best taxonomy of the world of strategic planning was developed by Henry Mintzberg, Bruce Ahlstrand, and Joseph Lampel (1998). Their book, *Strategy Safari: A Guided Tour Through the Wilds of Strategic Management,* is the premier guidebook to strategic planning because of the depth and breadth of its survey of the field. The book reviews the strengths and failings of the diverse approaches to strategic management and offers an objective and sometimes brutal assessment of each of the different schools of thought regarding strategic planning. Any leader or leadership team deciding to initiate a strategic-planning process should read this book before beginning their efforts.

In *Strategy Safari* the authors highlighted what they viewed as the 10 "schools" or broad approaches to strategic management. The schools that these authors identified and a brief description of each school's primary focus are featured in table 2–1.

What to Do Next

- ◆ Explore the diverse approaches to strategy formation highlighted in this chapter. Make an assessment of the best approach or combination of approaches for your organization.

- ◆ Begin thinking about the organizational environment in which you will be conducting the training.

- ◆ Review the next chapter to identify methods for gathering diverse perceptions of the organization, its leaders, and its employees.

- ◆ Begin developing some initial thoughts on the best approaches for reaching your target audience.

◆ ◆ ◆

The next chapter offers a number of strategies for assessing strategic-planning readiness in the organization and for identifying some of the competencies that are the focus for your training and development efforts. You'll consider three conventional approaches to assessment (interviews, focus groups, and written surveys) and learn a relatively new approach (appreciative inquiry) for better understanding the organization's climate and the skills that you'll be developing in your training.

Table 2-1

Approaches to Strategic Management

SCHOOL	PRIMARY APPROACH/FOCUS
Design school	Views strategy formation as a process of *conception*—usually by the leadership. This includes rationally assessing the environment and then developing the organizational strategies that provide the best customized fit with that environment. The leaders define the best strategy for the organization based on a profound awareness of the environment (using the SWOT analysis) and finally a conceptual and creative act of inventing the grand strategy. Key text: Andrews, 1987.
Planning school	Views strategy formation as a *formal*, step-by-step process. Largely done by "planners" (vs. leaders) who carefully manage the process through a formal and deliberate approach that sets broad strategic objectives (based on an environmental scan) and then decomposes these objectives into detailed subgoals and substrategies. The entire process of planning, budgeting, programming, and implementation is brought together into a master plan that guides the organization through its controls. Key text: Ansoff, 1965.
Positioning school	Views strategy formation as an *analytical* process. This school sees strategy as a process for deciding among a narrow range of options based on the economic marketplace. These few *generic* strategies (for example, product differentiation) were selected within the strategic-planning process through a careful analysis of the market and the capacities of the organization. Within this school, analysts and planners play a critical role by providing information to the managers and leaders who make the strategic choices. Key text: Porter, 1980.
Entrepreneurial school	Views strategy formation as a *visionary* process. This approach argues that strategy emerges from the entrepreneurial leader as an intuitive judgment based on the leader's wisdom, experience, and insight. This approach also allows for flexible adaptation as the leader's vision evolves in response to emerging conditions and issues. Key text: numerous books and articles about the leader's role in organizational transformation.
Cognitive school	Views strategy formation as a *mental* process. This school contends that strategy results from the cognitive process that takes place within the mind of the leader/strategist. The main argument of this school is that the leader's responses to the inputs from the environment (and the conceived strategies, as a result) are shaped by the leader's existing concepts, maps, schemas, mental models, and frames. Because the focus of this school is less on *what* strategy is developed and more on *how* the strategist develops strategy and what influences this cognitive process, this

Learning school

school is less prescriptive about the planning process. It simply identifies the key components of the strategists' cognitive process of strategy creation. Key text: Simon, 1977.

Views strategy as an *emergent* process. The major contribution of this school for strategic management is a focus on *how* strategies form (where they come from) and evolve over time. In a complex and unpredictable world, deliberate strategies and strategic control are impossible, according to this school. The only option is to focus on learning over time in response to emergent issues. The leader's role is diminished—recognizing that critical knowledge is diffused throughout the organization—while the collective system takes on a prominent role. There are multiple strategists making decisions and taking action in response to what is happening in the present. With this approach, the difference between strategy formulation and implementation disappears and the leader acts as a facilitator of organizational learning. Key texts: Argyris and Schon, 1978; Senge, 1990.

Power school

Views strategy formation as a process of *negotiation*. This school's approach to strategy recognizes that strategy formulation is all about power and influence in organizations. It contends that there are two levels of organizational power (micro power and macro power) and that each has an influence on organizational strategy. With *micro* power, organizational strategy emerges from the shifting levels and areas of influence (through persuasion, bargaining, negotiating, game playing, coalition building, and so forth), with the "winner" deciding organizational strategy—until the next shift in micro power. With *macro* power, the organization sets strategy to use its power and influence to actively shape the environment and the marketplace. It wields its macro power through control, cooperation, coalition building, forging alliances, and so forth. Key texts: Allison, 1971; Pfeffer and Salancik, 1978.

Cultural school

Views strategy formation as a *collective* process. This school sees the formation of strategy as a result of social interactions based on the beliefs, values, assumptions, mental models, myths, and understandings of the members of the organization. These characteristics of culture shape how the individuals view the world, take in information, form judgments, and make strategic decisions. The cultural school contends that the deliberate strategies that emerge from this social/cultural process tend to reinforce and preserve existing assumptions and perspectives—therefore often perpetuating existing strategies rather than inventing new ones. Key texts: Norman, 1977; Rhenman, 1973.

Environmental school

Views strategy as a *reactive* process. Whereas the other schools see the external environment as *a* factor in the formulation of strategy, this school views the environment as *the* factor. Proponents

continued on next page

Table 2–1, continued

Approaches to Strategic Management

SCHOOL	PRIMARY APPROACH/FOCUS
	see the organization (and its strategy) as reacting to these environmental forces. The failure of an organization to effectively understand and respond to these external forces leads to a process of natural selection: It dies. Within a context where the environmental forces are strong and powerful, an organization's leaders have little choice but to react. Although other schools always factor in the environment (using SWOT analysis, for example) as a force to be incorporated into a plan, this school postulates that the environment essentially determines the plan—that leaders, strategists, and others in the organization simply respond to whatever threats or opportunities the environment poses. Key text: Hannan and Freeman 1977.
Configuration school	Views strategy formation as a process of *transformation*. This school is an integrative one: It brings together the insights and approaches of all of the other schools within a framework that acknowledges the contributions and limitations of each. The premise of this school is that organizations experience long periods of stasis or equilibrium—where the organization's strategy is a perfect fit within its environment—followed by periods of transformation—where the organization may undergo a dramatic shift or realignment toward another, more effective configuration. The key to strategic management, argues this school, is to maintain stability in strategy when appropriate while being open and receptive to transformation. This school honors the other schools by drawing, when necessary, from intuitive leaders, formal planning processes, collective and individual learning, coalition building, responding to the environment, and so forth. Key texts: Miles and Snow, 1978; Mintzberg, 1978.

Chapter 3

Assessing Organizational Readiness for Strategic Planning

What's in This Chapter?

- Discussion of the importance of an environment conducive to strategic planning and thinking

- Explanation of strategic-planning organizational readiness assessment

- Enumeration of the core strategic-planning and -thinking competencies needed by leaders and staff

Strategic planning is never conducted in a vacuum. There is always an organizational and cultural context within which it occurs and this context plays a central role in the success of your efforts. Equally important and closely related is the mental mindset of leaders and staff. Their perspective on planning and their experience with the organization's use of the practice and process of planning influence whether they embrace or shun strategic-planning efforts. Finally, the skills and knowledge levels of the organization's leaders and staff have a direct bearing on both their acceptance of their role in strategy formulation and their ability to carry out this role successfully.

Assessing these organizational readiness issues—organizational and cultural context, the mental mindset of leaders and staff, and core strategic planning and thinking competencies—is your first order of business before you design and deliver your training program. With foreknowledge and a better understanding of these readiness factors, your process will be more effective at doing what it must do: preparing the organization for the challenges of the future and improving its performance.

An additional benefit to conducting a thorough needs analysis (perhaps even more valuable than identifying the skill and knowledge competencies that the organization will need to support strategic planning) is that the results can and should be used in designing and leading the strategic-planning process. As you'll see when we get to our discussion of assessment methods and the questions we encourage you to explore, the data you gather should be used in the design of the planning process itself. This information, which is crucial to the success of the process, will enable you to leverage your HRD role in the strategic planning process and strengthen your strategic partnership with the organization's top leadership.

Assessing the organization's readiness for strategic planning and decision making involves three core strategies: in-depth interviews with key stakeholders in the planning process, focus groups to explore cultural and mindset issues, and written or online surveys to assess organizational climate and staff mindsets.

In-Depth Interviews with Key Stakeholders

In-depth interviews with key stakeholders in the strategic-planning process will enable you to explore the diverse issues that make up organizational readiness. During these structured one-on-one interviews you can explore the respondents' mindsets as well as the organizational context issues of culture and the respondents' perceptions of the organization's planning history.

At a minimum you should plan on interviewing all of the members of the executive leadership team—the group often charged with leading strategic-planning efforts. You also should dig deeper into the organization by talking with a diverse sample of managers, supervisors, team leaders, and staff at every level. The point of your interviews is to discover how these various players view the organization and its capacities for long-range planning.

Each of your interviews should be structured so that you ask the same questions of all participants. Each interview should last no more than an hour and should provide an opportunity for participants to offer both their thoughts in response to your questions and further thoughts in the context of the interview's focus. Following the interviews you should summarize the results by noting the key themes and trends that surfaced in your discussions.

In crafting your questions, we recommend you use a process that reflects the Appreciative Inquiry (AI) method, a powerful technique developed by David Cooperrider in the 1980s that captures the organization's strengths and capabilities. Cooperrider asserted that those assets will enable an organization to effectively prepare for and respond to its current and future challenges. AI is grounded on two key assumptions. The first, and most important, is that organizations are sustained by what they do well, by their strengths and successes, and by the affirmative contributions that employees make at all levels toward the organization's success. The second assumption is that the nature of an inquiry itself—the kinds of questions that we ask and how we ask them—will influence how the individuals in the organization respond. Hence, by exploring the organization's strengths in your inquiry you will identify that which gives it life and will begin the subtle and positive shifting of perspective toward an affirmative strategic-planning process.

According to Cooperrider, Whitney, and Stavros (2003), AI is the "cooperative and co-evolutionary search for the best in people, their organizations, and the world around them. It involves the discovery of what gives 'life' to a living system when it is most effective, alive, and constructively capable in economic, ecological, and human terms" (p. 3).

A comprehensive AI process (which can involve dozens if not hundreds of interviews and includes both small- and large-group processes) can be a powerful foundation for the organization's strategic-planning efforts. The results can, in fact, drive key strategies, largely because of the participatory "discovery" process used and the rich reservoir of knowledge that often lies buried in the organization. You can, however, use a more eclipsed process modeled on the AI method. Although you won't reap the benefits of the more expansive process, what you learn from the more focused effort can and should play an important role in developing the overall strategic-planning and decision-making initiative.

Here are some suggested AI questions:

1. Reflect on this organization's history of thinking and planning for the future and tell me a story or cite an incident in which, from your perspective, this organization effectively and powerfully engaged in strategic thinking and/or planning.

   a. What enabled the strategic-thinking/planning process or event to go so well?

   b. What did the key players (stakeholders) do that enabled this successful outcome?

   c. What was it about the climate in the organization (or its subunit) that supported, reinforced, and sustained these strategic-thinking/planning efforts?

2. From your perspective, what do you see as the overarching vision for this organization? What should we seek to accomplish or create as a result of our work? What is the profoundly positive difference we should strive to make in the world?

3. What are the strengths of this organization in relation to its strategic thinking, planning, decision making, problem solving, and implementation? How have these strengths been expressed? How are they evident or visible?

4. What are the core values that should govern the way this organization engages in strategic thinking, planning, decision making, and implementation?

5. What do you think is the "life-giving" factor, value, or characteristic that enables this organization to pull through during difficult times?

6. How could this organization build on its strengths, core values, and life-giving factors to enable it to successfully think, plan, decide, and implement strategically—and to achieve its vision?

7. What current practices might this organization strengthen or develop to enable it to understand and effectively respond to the challenges ahead—and so achieve its strategic vision?

8. Imagine that it is one year from now and this organization has created and is actively implementing a strategic plan that moves it toward its strategic vision. How did the organization create this plan? How did the planning process engage key stakeholders (for example, leaders, staff, customers, and suppliers)? How did people work together at all levels of this organization to make the plan relevant and engaging? And as a result of this planning process, in what ways are people working, communicating, interacting, deciding, planning, and collaborating that differ from how it was before the process?

9. If I were to grant you three wishes that would help the organization achieve this successful and transformative strategic-thinking, -planning, and decision-making end result, what would those three wishes be?

10. Is there anything else you'd like to share with me that might help develop an effective and engaging strategic-planning process?

Answers to your AI-based questions will help you identify the organizational assets to build on when initiating your planning process. Although the questions will generate data that can be used to design your HRD programs, it is perhaps even more important that the insights from these interviews can be used by your strategic-planning design team (or whatever group will be guiding the process) to shape the way that the process and its outcomes unfold. These interview questions will lead you to some powerful insights into the organization's culture, practices, and behaviors. You and others can use these insights as building blocks for the larger planning process.

Focus Groups

Moving beyond the one-on-one interviews, focus groups enable you to explore in a group setting issues of strategic thinking, planning, and implementation and the skills people might require to do these things well. The group process enables a more interactive format in which individuals' ideas draw responses from and are tested by others in the group. You can ask questions similar to those used in the one-on-one interviews, or you can explore a different set of issues.

The greatest value of a group process in exploring these questions emerges from the ability to gather data on a group's reactions to each other's comments. The interactivity within the group and the opportunity to explore these issues in greater depth are the strongest selling points for using focus groups. As with the interviews, you should draw your participants from a diverse cross-section of the organization. Whether you create groups that are homogeneous (similar in kind) or heterogeneous (diverse and dissimilar), each group should be asked the same set of core questions with the opportunity for deeper exploration if needed. As it was with your interviews, your primary goal in analyzing the focus group data is to identify the broad trends in what people are saying. The results can form the basis for designing both your training program and the strategic-planning process itself.

Written Surveys

The written survey (whether distributed and completed online or using paper and pencil) provides a relatively inexpensive way to gather information from a large number of organizational stakeholders. As with the other forms of data gathering identified in this chapter, you should ensure that you have sampled a diverse cross-section of the organization. This increases your confidence that you can generalize findings to the whole entity. Although it is the most effective approach for reaching the greatest number of people, the written survey suffers from an inability to interact with the respondent in real time. It isn't easy to ask a follow-up or clarifying question or to explore additional ideas that surface in people's responses.

For all of these forms of data gathering, the quality of the questions, the diversity and distribution of the sample of people you involve, and how you analyze the data determine the actual quality and usefulness of the data. Although we recommend that you use all three approaches in your research leading to the strategic-planning process, you should select your approach based on what information you want to collect, how much interaction you want with your participants, the importance of gathering information from as many people as possible, and how much time and how many resources you have available.

Guidelines for Choosing Questions to Explore in Your Research

The questions you decide to explore depend on how you plan to use the data. If the only purpose of your needs analysis is to gather information to help you prepare for skill- and knowledge-building workshops, then your research will focus more narrowly than if your goal is to help inform the planning process itself.

The questions that follow, organized by area of exploration, can be modified for inclusion in any method you use to collect data. You also may want to infuse the focus group and written surveys with an AI orientation as highlighted earlier in the interview section of this chapter.

ASSESSING ORGANIZATIONAL READINESS FOR STRATEGIC PLANNING

Any of the data-gathering methods we've discussed here can be used to explore the issue of organizational readiness. In researching that area your focus is on the organization's culture and climate and the extent to which they conflict with or reinforce strategic-thinking and -planning methodologies. Here are some questions that enable you to investigate this issue:

◆ What do you see as the major challenges facing this organization over the next five years?

◆ What are the likely consequences for us if we don't effectively respond to these challenges?

◆ On a 10-point scale (1 = not at all; 10 = quite a bit), indicate your level of agreement with each of the following statements:

   a. Employees are quickly able to adjust to changes in this organization.

   b. The environment here is one where tradition and status quo define how people work.

   c. When things get stressful here, people tend to help each other (vs. only helping themselves).

   d. The organization's leadership has done a good job of communicating during past changes.

   e. When employees here have unanswered questions about a proposed organizational change, they are encouraged to ask these questions.

   f. The employees here are accustomed to making decisions on their own.

   g. Employees are encouraged to share their ideas about how to improve the quality of work life here.

   h. When things go wrong, we tend to focus on exploring the causes of the problem rather than on assigning blame.

   i. Employees tend to be intimidated by those who have power.

   j. Developing strategies to help the organization deal with the challenges of today and tomorrow is the sole responsibility of our executive leadership team.

◆ What, if any, issues and concerns do you have about how this organization engages in strategic planning and implementation?

◆ Where could the leaders here most improve in their ability to lead a strategic-planning process?

◆ To what extent do employees demonstrate strategic thinking in their daily work? Give examples.

◆ Describe your experience with planning (strategic or otherwise) in this organization. On balance, do you view this experience as a positive or negative one?

◆ What could this organization do to reinforce strategic thinking and planning in how employees approach their daily work?

ASSESSING STRATEGIC PLANNING COMPETENCIES

The skill and knowledge competencies that support strategic planning are best assessed through focus groups and written surveys. Possible questions include these:

◆ What skills and knowledge should our leaders develop to enable them to effectively create and implement a strategic plan for the organization?

◆ What skills and knowledge should employees develop to enable them to deal more effectively with the changes facing the organization in the years ahead?

◆ Using a 10-point scale (1 = not at all; 10 = quite a bit), answer each of the following questions:

How skilled is this organization's leadership in

  a. selling the importance of and need for making changes in the way the organization does business?

  b. encouraging employee participation in designing the way we work?

  c. encouraging employee participation in decision making?

  d. challenging employees to be strategic thinkers—thinking on behalf of the organization's future?

  e. listening to employees' ideas and concerns?

  f. responding to employees' issues and concerns about changes in organizational direction, policies, procedures, and practices?

◆ Using a 10-point scale (1 = not at all; 10 = quite a bit), answer each of the following questions:

How skilled are employees in

  a. asking clarifying questions about a coming change?

b. seeing the organization's big picture and its future (vs. focusing only on their own jobs or work lives)?

c. sharing their ideas for improving the organization, its systems, and its processes?

d. constructively resolving conflict between individuals and work groups?

e. making decisions and solving problems today with the long-range future of the organization in mind?

◆ What are the best methods for developing or strengthening the strategic-thinking, planning, decision-making, and implementation skills and knowledge you have identified?

ASSESSING THE CLARITY OF THE PLANNING PROCESS AND OUTCOMES

These questions should be directed at those who are initiating or leading the strategic-planning process in the organization. We recommend that these questions be explored with the strategic-planning design team more as a focus of a provocative discussion than for the purpose of data collection. Here are some questions that will provoke such a conversation:

◆ What are the business factors driving the need to develop the organization's strategic plan at this time? What's the business case for dedicating organizational resources to this initiative?

◆ To what extent do organizational stakeholders have a shared vision of the future for the organization?

◆ What do you see as the end results or outcomes when the strategic plan is developed? Will the plan be a living document that evolves and changes over time? Or is it expected to define a specific strategy that will remain largely unchanging over the life of the plan?

◆ Who will be involved in developing the strategic plan and how will they be involved? How will employees at every level be meaningfully engaged in the planning process?

◆ What, if any, objections to developing a strategic plan do you expect to hear from others? What experience suggests that you're likely to hear these objections?

◆ What strengths does this organization have that enable it to successfully create a strategic plan? How can the planning process build on these strengths?

◆ How can the strategic plan strengthen strategic thinking in the daily work of every employee? How should we develop and reinforce strategic thinking in employees?

◆ When the plan is finalized and implemented, what organizational systems and processes (for example, performance management, information systems, reward systems) will help sustain the plan and the strategic thinking by employees who support the plan?

◆ How will the plan be integrated into the organization's annual operational planning and budgeting process?

◆ Who will monitor the plan's implementation and take the lead in keeping the plan vital and responsive to a changing environment?

◆ What role is the top leadership expected to play in formulating, communicating, and promulgating the organization's vision, core values, and strategic agenda?

◆ What is your plan for communicating the planning process and final strategy to all stakeholders? How will these stakeholders stay abreast of progress and needed adjustments as the plan evolves?

◆ How will emergent issues be incorporated into the plan? And how will changes made to the plan that reflect these emergent issues be communicated to stakeholders?

◆ How can individuals at any level of the organization influence the plan after it moves into implementation?

◆ In general, how will the positive energy and vitality of the planning process and the final vision and strategic plan be sustained?

What to Do Next

◆ Develop your needs-assessment and data-collection strategies to help you identify HRD's role in shaping the strategic-planning process and developing the skills and knowledge required by managers, supervisors, and employees throughout the organization.

◆ Work closely with the strategic-planning design team to ensure that they are asking the right questions of themselves, that the data you gather are used within the planning process, and that your findings are integrated into the design of your training program.

◆ Review the next chapter to learn how to design training programs that develop the skills and knowledge organizational stakeholders will need to create an effective strategic plan.

◆ ◆ ◆

You're now ready to begin piecing together your strategic-planning training programs. The next chapter offers you some ideas and approaches for effective program design.

The Basics of Training Program Design

What's in This Chapter?

- The secret to designing an effective training program

- How to define your training outcomes, topics, and learning objectives

- How to develop your teaching points and match your training activities to them

- How to evaluate the overall flow and learning integration

- How to evaluate, pilot-test, and revise your workshop design

Designing a training program that delivers great results requires a thoughtful, disciplined approach toward your topic. Even with this book and CD in hand—with all of its learning modules, handouts, PowerPoint slides, exercises, and transitions—you will need to invest considerable time and energy to build the kind of training program that delivers on the organization's expectations and achieves your desired outcomes. This book is a starting place. The process of making it *your* program requires a careful application of good training design methods. In building a training program—or customizing any of the workshops in this book—you must identify

- what outcomes or deliverables you want the training to achieve for participants and for the organization

- the core competencies that the training will develop or reinforce to enable participants and the organization to achieve the desired outcomes

- the best way to teach those competencies

- how you will measure whether the learning outcomes were achieved.

This chapter offers you a road map for translating the workshops and materials into effective training that is appropriately customized around the needs, aspirations, expectations, limitations, constraints, and culture of the organization.

The Secret to Effective Design

Designing an effective training program is simple and elegant and complex and frustrating. It's simple and elegant in that the step-by-step process is relatively straightforward and easy to follow and it flows naturally toward an integrated "package" that you can call your training program. It's complex and frustrating in that good training design involves integrating the results of your needs analysis (some of which are conflicting and contradictory), being forced to make hard choices on what to include in and exclude from your design, and creating a flexible design that delivers required content while it adjusts to and accommodates emergent issues and topics during the session.

Even if you do everything right with training program design, there is no guarantee that learning will occur or that the results you hope for will be realized. When you "go live" anything can (and does!) happen—some of which reinforces learning and some of which takes away from it. Good training program delivery starts with a solid and thoughtful foundation the trainer builds on to accomplish what the organization expects and what the people who attend the session require. The secret to an effective program is thoughtful structure, organized learning, adaptable design, and an instructor with a "building-the-road-as-we-travel-it" openness to emergent issues.

So, let's start with the thoughtful structure for training program design.

Fundamentals of Effective Design

The training program design process comprises five stages of development: (1) defining your desired outcomes, teaching topics, and learning objectives; (2) developing your key teaching points; (3) identifying your methods and activities for each teaching point; (4) assessing the flow and integration of learning; and (5) evaluating and revising your program. As you'll see, this process, although simple, has its complexities and incorporates the results from your needs analysis. It's best to pull together a group of people to work as a design team in bringing your training program to life.

Let's look at the actions that you and your design team will need to take in each of these five areas.

DEFINE YOUR DESIRED OUTCOMES, TEACHING TOPICS, AND LEARNING OBJECTIVES

1. **Define the key organizational outcomes you hope to achieve through the training program.** You can get at this definition by answering some or all of these questions: What are the organizational end results that this training program is intended to achieve or influence? What is the business case for this program? What are the outcomes you'd like the training to accomplish for the organization? The results of your needs analysis can be helpful here.

2. **Define the performance outcome(s) that the training participants are expected to achieve.** You can get at this definition by answering some or all of these questions: What will the participants be able to accomplish or achieve as a result of the learning that occurs during the workshop? Again, your needs analysis results can be useful in defining these desired outcomes.

3. **Identify the core attitudes, skills, and knowledge that participants should learn in order to achieve both individual and organizational outcomes.** Based on your needs analysis, what core attitudes (*their affect*), skills (*their behaviors*), and knowledge (*their cognitive understandings*) should participants acquire through the training program? These are the three types of learning that become the target of your training program—the ABCs. Check to see that each type of learning relates to at least one of the organizational or participant outcomes (from steps 1 and 2 above). The ABCs must become the driving focus for your training program because if your program delivers on them, you're more likely to achieve your broader training outcomes.

4. **Identify topics for learning.** With your outcomes and the ABCs in mind, brainstorm all of the possible topics that could be included in the course you are teaching. Don't edit your thoughts. Ensure that you have identified topics that address the ABCs.

5. **Select the most important topics.** This is all about making tough choices. You have only a limited amount of time to deliver results so you must make careful selections. Look at your brainstormed list of topics and ask yourself which topics are the *most important* things that need to be learned. Your needs analysis can be helpful here but you may want to have additional conversations with the or-

ganization's leaders, managers, employees, potential participants, and other key stakeholders to ensure that you are focusing on the right topics and issues. After you've gathered more data, rank your list of topics in descending order. From this rank-ordered list, focus the balance of your design efforts on those topics at the top.

6. **Write learning objectives.** For each topic that you choose as essential for the workshop, write a learning objective that indicates what specific outcomes will be realized from the training. Each learning objective should include an action verb (see table 4–1) and a result. Each objective should complete this statement: *As a result of attending this course, participants will be able to....* Here are some examples:

    ◆   *analyze the external environment in which the company operates.*

    ◆   *develop a plan for assessing stakeholder expectations.*

    ◆   *create a vision statement for their work area or team.*

    ◆   *coordinate implementation of the strategic plan.*

DEVELOP YOUR KEY TEACHING POINTS

With your outcomes, topics, and learning objectives clearly defined, your next design step is to develop teaching points—the key things you want participants to learn in order to achieve the desired workshop outcomes.

1. **Define your teaching points.** For each learning objective that you have written, identify one or more teaching points. Ideas for these teaching points can come from the list of the key attitudes, behaviors, and knowledge areas you identified in the previous stage of the process. During the actual workshop, you will teach to these key points. The assumption, of course, is that delivering these points to the learners will directly lead to their learning the right things— things that support the objectives and outcomes of the course.

2. **Define learning type.** The next step involves identifying the type of learning that is the focus for each teaching point. As we discussed above, the three types of learning are *affective* (attitudes and beliefs), *behavioral* (skills), and *cognitive* (knowledge). Next to each teaching point, write the type of learning it addresses (A = affective, B = behavioral, and C = cognitive). You'll use the ABC designation later when it comes to matching the best activity or exercise to facilitate the teaching.

Table 4–1

Action Verbs to Use in Defining Your Learning Objectives

adopt	collect	demonstrate	establish	inspect	secure
advise	compile	describe	estimate	interpret	select
analyze	concur	design	evaluate	list	solve
approve	conduct	develop	facilitate	negotiate	specify
assemble	consolidate	direct	formulate	perform	supervise
assess	contribute	discuss	furnish	plan	train
assist	coordinate	display	guide	practice	verify
authorize	create	disseminate	illustrate	prevent	
calculate	define	enable	implement	process	
change	delegate	ensure	initiate	report	

3. **Limit yourself to no more than five or six teaching points for each learning objective.** If you have fewer than six you may have combined two objectives into one (for example, *describe and apply the steps of employee assessment* is actually two objectives). Here's an example of an objective and the teaching points that support it:

Learning Objective: As a result of attending this workshop on strategic decision making, participants will be able to analyze the root causes of a problem.

Teaching Points:

◆ Decision makers need to stop and reflect on causes before moving toward solutions or decisions. (B)

◆ People's beliefs often prompt them to skip this analysis and leap to solutions and decisions. (A)

◆ There are specific tools and methods that assist in analyzing the root causes. (C)

◆ These are the ways to use or apply those tools and methods to a specific PSDM situation. (B)

◆ Be careful that the decision or problem statement doesn't imply a cause. (A)

4. **Talk to your sources.** With your learning objectives and teaching points defined, talk with some of the people you met with earlier (as

part of your needs analysis). Verify that you and the design team have identified the most important training topics and the right learning objectives, and that the teaching points drive home the correct lessons or learning. This check-up is important because the next step involves the labor-intensive process of developing the activities, sequence, and flow for the workshop.

MATCH YOUR TEACHING METHODS
TO YOUR TEACHING POINTS

Now for the first time in the design process you'll identify what you will *do* during the workshop. Here you need to draw on your repertoire of training activities and methods and then match the best method or technique to each teaching point. You'll deal with the overall time of the activities and the length of the workshop in the next stage. For this stage, your focus is on developing the best methodology to achieve your learning objectives.

1. **Focus on one learning objective at a time.** For each teaching point, select the most appropriate teaching method or technique based on the type of learning (A, B, or C) that should occur. (Table 4–2 connects various teaching methods or activities with the type of learning each tends to support.) Be aware that one training activity or technique may be used for a number of teaching points (for example, role playing can address affective, behavioral, *and* cognitive teaching points). Pay particular attention to the strengths and weaknesses of each activity or technique when making your match.

2. **Write the appropriate technique next to the teaching point.** For each of your teaching points, identify the specific activity or technique that you'll use to deliver the point.

3. **Assess whether all of your techniques work together to support the learning objectives.** After you have finished identifying all of the techniques you'll use to teach all of the points for a learning objective, decide if the techniques work well together. Make changes and adjustments as necessary to seamlessly integrate teaching points and methods.

4. **Establish a sequence for the techniques.** Take an arm's-length perspective on the sequence of training techniques and methods. At this point you're looking for the right feeling and flow to the learning process. Some of the things you'll be looking for include

Table 4–2

The ABCs of Training Techniques

TRAINING TECHNIQUE	DESCRIPTION	ATTITUDE	BEHAVIOR	COGNITION
Brainstorming	Rapid-paced group generation of numerous ideas			✓
Buzz group	Short (five-minute) team discussion of specific topic	✓		✓
Case study	Written/video case analyzed by individuals or groups	✓		✓
Circle of knowledge	Team round-robin recording; team strives for consensus	✓		✓
Circle response	Group (8–10) sits in circle; each person offers quick comment to question/issue raised by trainer	✓		✓
Critical incident	Class reacts to and analyzes situation posed by trainer	✓	✓	✓
Debate	Teams develop their strategy and then debate different sides of an issue	✓	✓	✓
Demonstration	Trainer demonstrates ideal behaviors; group discusses reactions and offers suggestions	✓		✓
Field trip	Learners are asked to venture outside the training room to learn, observe, assess, and evaluate a specific environment	✓	✓	✓
Fishbowl	Group process that involves an *inner* group discussing a topic and an *outer* group observing the interactions of the inner group; facilitator moves people into and out of the circles or establishes rules for such movement	✓	✓	
Game	Participants apply/demonstrate the lessons in a game situation (for example, games modeled on television shows such as *Jeopardy, Match Game, Hollywood Squares,* and so forth)	✓	✓	✓
Group inquiry	Team members read a handout; group develops questions and strives to answer each question themselves	✓		✓
Guided teaching	Trainer asks a question of the large group to provoke exploration; records responses on a flipchart	✓		✓

continued on next page

Table 4-2, continued

The ABCs of Training Techniques

TRAINING TECHNIQUE	DESCRIPTION	ATTITUDE	BEHAVIOR	COGNITION
Icebreaker	Tool to help integrate the participant into the learning topic, with the team, the full group, or both	✓		✓
Information research	Members are directed to find information on their own by exploring specific resources available to them	✓	✓	✓
Computer- or Internet-based activity	Training directed by learner through a structured learning experience	✓	✓	✓
Learning contract	Participants write contracts for learning	✓		
Learning journal	Learners write out personal insights, applications, and goals	✓		✓
Lecture/mini-lecture	Learners listen to key teaching points			✓
Mental imagery	Trainer guides members with mental images	✓	✓	
Observation	Participants are directed to observe an event and be prepared to share reflections/reactions/insights	✓	✓	✓
Physical continuum	Participants locate themselves on a line to express their relative position on an issue presented by the facilitator (for example, stress, confusion, joy, anxiety, and so forth)	✓		
Project	Teams are assigned a detailed task to complete	✓	✓	✓
Question board/ parking lot	Each participant has access to sticky-notes that he or she can use to post questions for the facilitator	✓		✓
Read and discuss	Participants read and reflect on a handout and discuss in teams	✓		✓
Role play	Individuals are assigned roles or they play themselves	✓	✓	
Self-assessment	Participants complete written self-assessments with interpretation facilitated by the trainer	✓	✓	
Simulation	Extended role play that recreates near reality	✓	✓	✓

Method	Description
Storytelling	Facilitator tells a story (out of his or her own experience or that of others) that explains key lessons/themes; alternative method is to have a participant tell a story from his or her own experience that relates to the topic at hand
Teaching teams	Learning team is charged with first learning something as a team and then teaching it to other teams
Video presentation	Participants view video, offer reactions, and ask questions
Writing task	Goal setting and action planning

- ◆ new learning that builds on previous learning

- ◆ the value or usefulness of behavior (practice) following cognition (presentation of the theory), or vice versa

- ◆ the time requirements for a single teaching point versus the time available for other important teaching points

- ◆ the movement from simple concepts to complex ones

- ◆ the transition from the concrete to the abstract.

Order the techniques from top to bottom across the entire learning objective—making sure that they match up with the appropriate teaching point.

EVALUATE THE OVERALL FLOW AND INTEGRATION OF LEARNING

The final stage of your up-front training program design involves assessing the overall structure and flow of your workshop design. You are also paying attention now to the overall sequence of learning and the extent to which your final design reflects the desired outcomes (for both participants and the organization) that you defined in the first stage of the design process.

1. **Make certain that your outcomes and objectives are met by the workshop design.** Look back at your original outcomes and learning objectives for the program. How well does the final design reflect the priorities you established at the outset? How likely is it that the activities you have proposed will deliver the key outcomes for the organization and for the participants?

2. **Verify that the overall learning path/structure works as a whole.** As you did for the individual learning outcomes, look at the sequencing and flow between topics and across the entire training program. Will learners experience natural transitions from one topic to another? Is the dedication and allocation of time appropriate—in other words, does the workshop give the most time to the most important topics and learning objectives?

3. **Make adjustments to the design to reflect the actual training time available.** You may find that you have eight hours of training activities to fill a workshop that's limited to six hours. Now is the time to make minor or major adjustments in your timing and perhaps even in the activities you decide to incorporate in the final

design. If you think it's impossible to teach a two-day course in three hours, you're right. In this step of the process you focus on scaling back or ramping up your design to match the time available. You may have to choose a different set of activities for your teaching points that either contracts or expands the time dedicated to the activity. At this step, if you decide to eliminate a learning objective and its related teaching points because of time constraints, refer to the topic prioritizing you did earlier to ensure that you continue to focus on the most critical items.

4. **Finalize your design.** Pull together your revisions into a final training program design that reflects the desired organizational and participant outcomes, associated training topics and learning objectives, the sequence and flow of the training activities, and the training time available.

EVALUATE, PILOT-TEST, AND REVISE YOUR TRAINING PROGRAM

1. **Identify what you want to measure.** Before you go live with your final training program design, take some time to identify specific methods within your design for evaluating both the training *process* (that is, how do the learners experience the session?) and its *outcomes* (that is, what have they learned?). We'll explore evaluation in greater detail in the next chapter, but it's important to view evaluation as a central component of design. For each training topic, you need to ask such questions as these:

    ◆ How will we know that learning has occurred? (*outcome*)

    ◆ How will we measure the effect of the training on the organization's performance? (*outcome*)

    ◆ How can we measure the quality and effectiveness of the way that the training program was designed? (*process*)

    ◆ How can we assess whether the participants' needs were addressed by the program? (*process*)

2. **Build outcome and process measures into the design.** For each of your key training topics and learning objectives, identify how you will measure whether learning occurred. These outcome measures can be done during the training (for example, by observation, quiz,

demonstration of learned behaviors, and so forth) or following the training (for example, by quiz, survey, reports from others, improved trainee performance, and improved organizational performance).

Process measures assess the skills of the trainer, the degree to which the training environment supported learning, and the relevancy of the training topics. They can be done during the training (via check-ins on how people are doing throughout the session, observation of body language and level of participation, and the like) or at the end of or following the training (with reaction sheets, follow-along surveys, and post-training debriefing with selected participants).

3. **Pilot-test your program.** If possible, try out your course on a select group of participants—those you know will give you honest and constructive feedback on process and flow issues as well as the overall deliverables of the workshop. This rehearsal (which may be the first time you offer the course or may be a special try-out session) ensures that when you roll out your program to the rest of the organization, there'll be few nasty surprises.

4. **Revise your program in line with pilot-test feedback.** Make the necessary adjustments and refinements in course design that become apparent through the dry-run feedback and through your own intuitive sense of how the course flowed. Although you should expect to further refine the techniques you use and the entire program as you go forward, we recommend that you *not* make major changes until after you've conducted at least several offerings of the workshop and gathered enough data to show what works and what doesn't.

5. **Don't let your training stagnate.** Even after you've settled on a workshop design that works, continue to gather performance data (both process and outcome) to ensure that the session continues to meet both the learner's and the organization's expectations. Making changes and adjustments to your workshop over time will not only improve its ability to deliver on the key outcomes that others care about; it also will make the course vital and fun for you to teach. By encouraging ongoing evaluation you move closer to achieving the results you and others hope for, and you can grow and learn along with your participants.

Some Last Thoughts on Good Design

Good training design is deeply anchored in the characteristics of adult learners and in creating a training environment that reinforces learning. Here are our final thoughts for building a training program that facilitates participant learning and achieves the organization's desired outcomes.

- ◆ **Emphasize the relevance and importance of the skills and knowledge being developed.** People are more likely to be open to learning if they see the connection between what you are teaching and their daily work.

- ◆ **Offer a moderate level of content.** The greatest danger for training designers is trying to do too much in the available time. We sometimes discover (often too late) that our perfect workshop design doesn't allow for the presence of real people with real questions. To escape this fate, be brutally selective in what you decide to include in your program. Separate what people *need* to know from what *would be nice* for them to know.

- ◆ **Balance the amount of ABC learning.** Too much focus on one form of learning over another can negatively affect the quality of the outcomes you want. People may learn an effective method for making decisions, such as the decision matrix (cognitive learning), but they may still have an attitude that says "I don't really need to involve others in the decision-making process" (affective learning). Ensure that you incorporate all three learning targets in your training by exploring and fostering attitudes, developing skills, and imparting knowledge and understanding.

- ◆ **Use a variety of teaching approaches.** Adults learn in different ways: through movement (kinesthetic methods), through sound (auditory methods), and through sight (visual methods). Mixing up your teaching methods and approaches helps sustain interest and increases the likelihood that you'll connect with the learner one way or another.

- ◆ **Build on the background and expertise of the learner.** Introduce learning that is connected in some way with what the learner already knows or has experienced. Learners bring a wealth of knowledge and experience to a training session. Honor this experience and encourage participants to learn from each other as much as they might learn from you.

◆ **Put participants in the driver's seat.** Adult learners want to be in charge of their own learning. Develop learning partnerships with workshop participants. Use role playing, case examples, simulations, and so forth as much as possible and lecture as little as possible.

◆ **Present real-life examples and problem solving.** Emphasize the real world as much as possible in every aspect of your training. Help learners build a bridge from the workshop to the workplace by offering problems, activities, and examples from their own experience. Demonstrate how learning will help them back on the job.

◆ **Provide opportunity for application back on the job.** An active training program builds in opportunities for participants to apply learning to real situations after the training program ends. Create learning contracts and action plans focused on encouraging the application of the learned skills and knowledge on the job.

◆ **Stay flexible and self-confident.** Remain confident in your work and your professional depth. You've done your research, you've tested your ideas, you've made adjustments. Have faith in what you've designed and move forward with confidence. If an activity fails during the workshop, know the signs, take a break (if necessary), caucus with yourself (and others?), and then shift gears accordingly. Follow participant needs and questions, stay true to both your objectives and your audience, and remain calm and confident. If you do these things, you're destined to do the right thing!

What to Do Next

◆ Begin preparing your strategic-planning and decision-making training sessions using the results from your needs analysis, the ideas from this chapter, and the suggested session designs in the chapters that follow.

◆ Adjust and modify the agendas and activities offered in this workbook to suit the objectives, audience, time available, and your own teaching style and preferences.

◆ Get approval and commitment for your proposed training program and its objectives from the organization's leaders.

◆ Practice. Debrief with selected participants to help you make adjustments to the training content and design.

◆ Join the local chapter of ASTD to pick up additional workshop design tips and tricks from others in the profession.

◆◆◆

You're not quite ready to go live with your program. As we explained in this chapter, you need to build evaluation into the heart of your training. Rather than making evaluation simply a reaction sheet at the end of the session, put some time into designing an evaluation process that gives you effective feedback on your training process and outcomes. So, let's move to the next chapter to learn more about building evaluation into your design and using the results from this evaluation to improve your training program.

Evaluating Your Training Program Results

What's in This Chapter?

♦ Discussion of the role of evaluation in assessing the effects of your training program

♦ Explanations of Kirkpatrick's four levels of evaluation

♦ Descriptions of approaches for measuring participant reactions, learning, behavior change, and organizational results

♦ Instructions for developing your evaluation methods

Gone are the days of taking the effectiveness of our training program at face value. In a time of lean operations and increasing demands for demonstrating the positive organizational impact from our training dollars, we must incorporate evaluation into the very heart of every one of our training programs. This chapter offers you a quick overview of training program evaluation and a few ideas that you can use to assess the multiple levels of your training program's effectiveness.

Any attempt to measure the value and effectiveness of your program must begin with the classical four levels of training evaluation developed by Donald Kirkpatrick in 1959. Described initially in a four-part series titled "Techniques for Evaluating Training Programs" in *Training Director's Journal* and more recently in his 1994 book, *Evaluating Training Programs: The Four Levels*, his evaluation levels continue to be the worldwide standard that almost all training evaluation efforts follow. Kirkpatrick's four levels are

♦ **Level 1—Participant Reaction and Intention:** This level of evaluation focuses on the reaction of participants to the training program. Although this is the lowest level of measurement, it remains an important dimension to assess. If people are unhappy with the learning environment, the instructor, the pace of the workshop, and so forth, they may be less able to learn what they need to learn.

◆ **Level 2—Participant Learning:** The concern of this assessment level is whether the participants actually learned what you expected them to learn as a result of attending the training session. This level measures the participant's acquisition of cognitive knowledge or behavioral skills as a result of the workshop. This could be demonstrated by a participant being able to describe strategic thinking and its core characteristics—or, in a decision-making workshop, by a participant demonstrating the correct use of a decision matrix in an in-class exercise.

◆ **Level 3—Participant Behavior Change:** This level focuses on the degree to which training participants are able to transfer their learning to their workplace behaviors. For example, if participants learned the characteristics of strategic thinking in your workshop, are they able to demonstrate strategic thinking behaviors back on the job?

◆ **Level 4—Impact and Results:** The last of Kirkpatrick's levels moves beyond the training participant to assess the *impact* of the training on organizational performance. For strategic-planning training, this would ask the fundamental question, Did a well-developed and -implemented strategic plan, based on the training provided, enable the organization to achieve its strategic objectives and goals?

ASTD's *2003 State of the Industry Report* presented benchmark data on the levels of evaluation practiced by organizations. Of the 276 organizations who completed surveys as part of ASTD's Benchmarking Service, 75 percent reported that they evaluated their training programs at Level 1 (reaction) and 41 percent indicated that they evaluated at Level 2 (learning). Only 21 percent of these organizations reported that they evaluated whether the training resulted in behavioral change (Level 3), and only 11 percent reported efforts to assess whether training led to organizational improvement or results (Level 4) (pp. 18–19).

Assessing the effectiveness of your training—at least the first three levels—should be an integral part of your training program design. Assessing Level 4, although less common because of the difficulty of measuring the cause-and-effect relationship between training and organizational outcomes, should also be undertaken to the extent that you are able. Table 5–1 highlights Kirkpatrick's

Table 5-1
Strategies for Evaluating Your Training Program

EVALUATION LEVEL	WHEN CONDUCTED	IDEAS AND STRATEGIES
1: Participant reaction and intention	During the training program and at the conclusion of the session	**During the session:** ◆ Use learning temperature or "pulse" reading cards (one word that describes what you're feeling/thinking/learning) ◆ Have participants post their reactions on flipchart pages: *Content and Methods* ◆ Observe: Are people engaged? Having fun? ◆ Hold a midcourse sharing of key insights (are they learning the right things?) ◆ Action planning: Ask about their *intentions* following the session? Do they take the action-planning process seriously? **At the end of the session:** ◆ Ask everyone to complete an end-of-program reaction sheet addressing learning environment, useful content and tools, areas for improvement, relevance of content, and so forth
2: Participant learning	During the training program and at the conclusion of the session	**During the session:** ◆ Observe: When you use role playing, case studies, presentations, and so forth, are people doing and saying things that reflect the content of the training? ◆ Action planning: Determine if participants' action plans reflect an integration of the course content **At the end of or following the session:** ◆ Use pre- and post-tests or quizzes to measure the participant's acquisition of core content ◆ Use follow-along surveys: What learning do participants report *following* the training?

continued on next page

Table 5-1, continued
Strategies for Evaluating Your Training Program

EVALUATION LEVEL	WHEN CONDUCTED	IDEAS AND STRATEGIES
3: Participant behavior change	Generally following the training session	**Following the session:** ◆ Use self-reports: Do participants report changes in attitudes and behaviors? ◆ Use surveys of others: Do the participants' supervisors, staff, or peers report changes in core-content attitudes and behaviors? ◆ Observe: Do participants demonstrate the new behaviors in their daily work?
4: Impact and organizational results	Following enough post-training time for Level 3 behavior change to have positive effects on organizational results	**Following the session:** ◆ Gather organizational data: Collect performance data on outcomes that are positively affected by the training's content. These outcomes might include reductions in employee turnover, fewer defects, less overtime, more on-time deliveries, higher customer satisfaction, less wait time for customer service, less machine downtime, increased sales, time-to-market data, and greater employee commitment to performance improvement. **Note:** Demonstrating the impact of training on organizational performance is a research question—one that demands a thoughtful process that uses proven social science research methodology. At a minimum, this requires that you track key organizational performance data *before* the training is offered. In addition, the best research design would establish a control group that didn't receive the training and then compare the performance differences between the trained and untrained groups. ◆ Use surveys or interviews with customers, supervisors, staff, peers, and other stakeholders ◆ Compare pre- and post-training performance outcomes ◆ Compare performance results of those who received training with those who did not

four levels, notes when each can and should be assessed, and suggests some possible strategies you can use to conduct your assessment.

Developing Your Evaluation Methods

Your assessment methods should be integrated into your training program design. This means that as you design your training program, you should identify specific opportunities and methods for assessing the various levels of evaluation outlined in this chapter.

To assist you with assessing Level 1, we have included a sample reaction sheet that you may find useful—Tool 12–4: Workshop Level 1 Evaluation (on the CD). For assessing Levels 2 and 3 you'll need to spend some time developing quizzes or tests to assess learning and identify a method to gather data on post-training behavior change. For assessing Level 4—the most difficult level to assess—you are encouraged to begin documenting the performance indicators that your training program intends to influence. You may also want to consider exploring the return-on-investment (ROI) for your training dollars. Calculating ROI, which is one means of measuring the impact of your training, can be a powerful way to document the contribution of training to your organization's long-term success.

Some of the best work in calculating ROI has been done by Jack L. Phillips. His efforts at highlighting the importance of ROI and providing some tools for doing so have made a significant contribution to the training world. His book *Return on Investment in Training and Performance Improvement Programs* (2003), is perhaps the best text on the process of calculating ROI and demonstrating the value of training. Other resources that might be useful in exploring ROI include ASTD's ROI Network (www.astd.org/ASTD/education_network) and the Jack Phillips Center for Research (www.franklincovey.com/jackphillips).

What to Do Next

- ◆ Design an approach for training evaluation that addresses all four levels.

- ◆ Review Tool 12–4 for possible assessment issues to include in your workshop evaluation process.

- ◆ Explore methods for calculating the ROI for your training program.

◆◆◆

The next chapter is the first of several that offer suggested workshop agendas for your training program on strategic planning and decision making. With your pre-work done and a plan for evaluation in place, you're ready to begin your workshop design.

One-Day Workshop: Fundamentals of Strategic Planning

What's in This Chapter?

- List of objectives for the one-day workshop on fundamentals of strategic planning

- Lists of materials for instructor and participants

- Detailed instructions on workshop preparation

- Workshop agenda and facilitator's guide

This chapter introduces the first of several workshops for your use in developing the strategic-planning, implementation, and decision-making competencies of managers and employees at every level of the organization. Because our philosophy of practice is that the world of strategy formation is *everyone*'s responsibility (not just that of the leadership team), all of the workshops included in this book are targeted toward both those who are leading and those who are participating in the strategic-planning and decision-making process. Our belief in employee involvement and participation in strategy formation places these frontline people at the very center of the process, although the final decision regarding key strategic direction may lie with the leadership team or the board of directors.

Mere participation in the process is no great virtue (to paraphrase W. Edwards Deming). It's an *informed participation for a specific purpose* that really makes the difference. For this reason, developing broad-based competencies in strategic planning and decision making at all levels of the organization should be one of the key objectives of your training program. To this end, the workshop designs of this and following chapters focus on building skills in these areas in employees on the front line as well as in those people in the executive boardroom.

Objectives

As a result of participating in this workshop, participants will be able to

- ◆ describe strategic planning and enumerate the common components of a strategic plan

- ◆ describe the role that strategic planning plays in enabling long-term success for any organization

- ◆ identify how strategic planning differs from other forms of organizational planning

- ◆ develop strategic-thinking skills in themselves and others

- ◆ work through the key stages of the strategic-planning process: (1) assess the current environment; (2) develop a vision of the future and define key governing values/beliefs; (3) identify strategic issues and develop action goals/plans; and (4) implement, monitor, and revise the plan

- ◆ identify methods for involving key stakeholders in strategy formulation and implementation

- ◆ describe common obstacles to strategic planning and ways to overcome them.

Materials

For the instructor:

- ◆ Projector, screen, and computer for running the PowerPoint slides

- ◆ PowerPoint slides 6–1 through 6–42

- ◆ Learning Activity 11–1: Ensuring Organizational Success

- ◆ Learning Activity 11–2: Perceptions of Strategic Planning

- ◆ Learning Activity 11–3: Definition and Key Components of Strategic Planning

- ◆ Learning Activity 11–4: Purpose and Goals of Strategic Planning

- ◆ Learning Activity 11–5: Value of Strategic Thinking

- ◆ Learning Activity 11–6: Levels of Planning in Organizations

- Learning Activity 11–7: An Integrated Model for Strategic Planning

- Learning Activity 11–8: Stages of Strategic Plan Development

- Learning Activity 11–9: Involving Stakeholders in the Strategic-Planning Process

- Learning Activity 11–10: Organizational Strengths to Support and Sustain Strategic Plan Implementation

- Tool 12–1: Training Room Configuration and Layout

- Tool 12–4: Workshop Level 1 Evaluation

- Tool 12–5: The Parking Lot

- Two flipcharts, easels, and marking pens for your use at the front of the room

For the participants:

- Tool 12–2: Goal-Setting Worksheet

- Tool 12–3: Ah-Ha! Sheet

- Handouts and training instruments needed in the learning activities

Using the CD

Materials for this training session are provided either in this workbook or as electronic files on the accompanying CD. To access the electronic files, insert the CD and click on the appropriate Adobe .pdf document or PowerPoint .ppt/.pps file. Further directions and help using the files can be found in the appendix, "Using the Compact Disc," at the back of this workbook. Thumbnail versions of the PowerPoint slides for this workshop (*Fundamentals.ppt/.pps*) are included at the end of this chapter.

Preparation

Several months before the workshop:

1. If appropriate, meet with representatives of the executive leadership team to discuss their expectations for this workshop.

2. Identify your target audience for this workshop, which serves as a stand-alone program for building basic knowledge and skills in front-

line staff and managers. (The next chapter presents an advanced issues in strategic planning workshop that builds on these fundamentals and is directed at those who are charged with developing or guiding the development of the strategic plan. Offered together as a two-day program, these two workshops provide an overview of the process [the fundamentals] and develop the more advanced skills to move the strategic-planning process forward.)

3. Schedule the session and arrange for a training room. If follow-on workshops are planned, schedule those sessions now. Ensure that the room can be configured to facilitate participant learning. See Tool 12–1 for a suggested room layout for the workshop.

4. Design the program around the organization's proposed strategic-planning process. Make sure that your training reflects the priorities and focus of the CEO and executive leadership group.

5. Prepare training materials and familiarize yourself with their content and operation.

6. Send an invitation memo, letter, or e-mail to participants, reiterating the purpose of the workshop and its importance in developing an effective strategic plan and effective strategic thinkers in the organization. It may be helpful to have this communication come from your CEO or chief operations officer to reinforce the significance and value of program participation.

7. Order food and beverages as necessary.

Just prior to the workshop:

1. Arrive early at the training room.

2. Check room setup and make needed adjustments.

3. Set up flipcharts and markers, and test equipment such as LCD and overhead projectors.

4. Prepare and post flipchart pages titled "Your Goals/Questions" and "Parking Lot" (Tool 12–5), if desired, and any additional flipchart pages detailed in the learning activities. You may also want to post another flipchart page highlighting key questions that relate to the objectives to be addressed during the workshop.

5. Display PowerPoint slide 6–1 as a welcome to participants and greet them individually as they enter the room.

Sample Agenda

8:30 a.m.   Welcome (5 minutes)

Welcome participants to the Fundamentals of Strategic Planning and Strategic Thinking Workshop. Introduce yourself. Point out the questions that you've posted on a flipchart:

1. How does an organization achieve a set goal?

2. What distinguishes successful companies from unsuccessful ones?

3. How does any organization successfully cope with the dramatic changes occurring in the marketplace, in consumer expectations, in technological advancements, and in the global economy?

4. What ensures the long-term success of an organization? (**Note:** This is the key question introducing the first learning activity.)

8:35   Learning Activity 11–1: Ensuring Organizational Success (25 minutes)

This activity quickly starts participants thinking about the big question—*How can we ensure an organization's long-term success?*—the fundamental question that strategic planning and strategic thinking try to answer.

9:00   Goal setting (30 minutes)

Make the transition from the opening activity by suggesting that today's workshop strives to address some of the historical problems with strategic planning while developing some core knowledge and skills to build a stronger, more effective organization for the future. Review the specific goals and road map for the day with slide 6–7.

Distribute Tool 12–2 and ask participants to identify

◆ their individual objective for the workshop, and how likely it is that they will realize that objective in this session

- what's in it for them if they achieve their objective, and how likely it is that the reward will materialize

- how important this positive benefit or reward is to them.

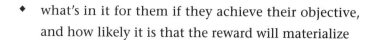

After a couple of minutes display slide 6–8 and ask participants to work in their small groups to (a) meet and greet, (b) share their personal objectives (the first of the questions on the Goal-Setting Worksheet), and (c) identify two to three questions about strategic planning and strategic thinking that the group would like to address during the workshop. Give the small groups approximately seven minutes for this activity.

Have the groups report their questions and record them on the prepared flipchart page. Highlight the importance of their taking responsibility for their own learning by exploring the answers to these questions as you work through the content of the session.

Point out that you have posted a Parking Lot as a place to record additional issues and questions that you may not be able to address today, and encourage them to post parking lot issues at any time.

Distribute Tool 12–3. Encourage them to be active participants in their own learning by using the Ah-Ha! Sheet to record key learning moments and the insights that will be most useful to them beyond today's session.

Note the schedule for breaks and lunch and the locations of restrooms, telephones, and refreshments.

9:30   Learning Activity 11–2: Perceptions of Strategic Planning (20 minutes)

Guide participants through this activity to identify how they define and view strategic planning from their own experiences.

9:50   Break (15 minutes)

10:05   Learning Activity 11–3: Definition and Key Components of Strategic Planning (20 minutes)

This brief lecture defines strategic planning and identifies the key components of a strategic plan.

10:25 Learning Activity 11–4: Purpose and Goals of Strategic Planning (20 minutes)

This buzz-group activity engages participants in identifying why strategic planning is useful to an organization.

10:45 Learning Activity 11–5: Value of Strategic Thinking (35 minutes)

Make a transition to this activity by noting that so far you've explained what strategic planning is and what a plan comprises. Note that planning, by itself, isn't enough to guide an organization into the future. Having strategic thinkers at all levels is even more important than having a strategic plan in place.

This learning activity develops insights into the role of strategic thinking in good strategic planning and organizational success.

11:20 Learning Activity 11–6: Levels of Planning in Organizations (40 minutes)

Continuing the exploration of strategic thinking and its role in organizations, this learning activity introduces participants to the four levels of planning in organizations (that is, *tactical, operational, interactive,* and *strategic*). Participants will identify how much time they currently spend at each of the levels—and how much time they believe they *should* spend at each level. The activity ends with participants identifying actions to take to "escape" from the tactical level.

Noon Lunch (60 minutes)

1:00 p.m. Learning Activity 11–7: An Integrated Model for Strategic Planning (15 minutes)

Tie together the earlier discussions of the components of strategic planning, the levels of organizational planning, and strategic thinking.

1:15   Learning Activity 11–8: Stages of Strategic Plan Development (60 minutes)

You introduce the four-stage strategic-planning process with this activity. After a quick overview of the process, participants work in small groups to identify the actions that organizational leaders and staff can take at all levels to accomplish the objectives of each stage.

2:15   Break (15 minutes)

2:30   Learning Activity 11–9: Involving Stakeholders in the Strategic-Planning Process (45 minutes)

Introduce this activity by noting that both strategy formulation (largely an intuitive process) and strategy implementation (largely a rational/analytical process) require the active participation of line workers and other stakeholders, in addition to the top leaders of an organization.

Participants identify which stakeholders should be involved in strategy formulation/implementation and how they should be involved. The key takeaway is an action plan for engaging the entire organization and its stakeholders in a meaningful strategic-planning process. If the organization has already identified various stakeholder groups and their potential involvement in planning, be sure to share this information during this activity.

3:15   Learning Activity 11–10: Organizational Strengths to Support and Sustain Strategic-Plan Implementation (45 minutes)

In this final activity, drawing on appreciative inquiry, participants identify the organization's competencies and strengths that will enable it to successfully develop and implement a strategic plan. The activity reveals some of the most common obstacles to a meaningful plan and guides participants in using the organization's strengths to address those obstacles.

4:00   Integration and conclusion (25 minutes)

Bring together the various elements of the workshop content and review the questions the group identified earlier in the day in the goal-setting segment. As time permits, ask participants to answer any unaddressed question, either in small groups or as a full class.

Display slide 6–41 and highlight these key points in your concluding remarks:

◆ Strategic planning plays an essential role in organizational life by clarifying what's important and focusing efforts at all levels of the organization.

◆ Developing strategic thinking at all levels is equal in importance to, or perhaps more important than, having a strategic plan. Strategic thinking enables employees to make daily decisions that are shaped by the vision and the strategic priorities identified in the strategic plan.

◆ The tactical and operational levels of planning tend to dominate our daily work because they both stare us in the face. The challenge for us is to ensure that these levels are informed and shaped by strategic planning and thinking.

◆ There are many approaches to strategic planning and a plan may take different forms. Each approach has its own advantages and disadvantages and each organization must choose the approach that best matches its culture and requirements.

◆ Participation by key stakeholders representing all levels of the organization helps ensure that the strategic plan (a) reflects the daily realities at the tactical level (experienced by customers and employees), (b) is imbued with the ideas and aspirations of more than just the leaders, and (c) is accepted by those who are expected to implement it at the operational and tactical levels.

Encourage them to take the next step and integrate into their daily work the various elements of the action plans they developed throughout the day.

If the advanced issues and methods workshop is planned, note the date of the session and set the expectation that the session will dig deeper into a variety of plan implementation issues and challenges.

4:25   Evaluation (5 minutes)

Display slide 6–42. Thank participants for attending the workshop and for being actively involved all day.

Distribute Tool 12–4 and encourage participants to leave the completed forms at their seats or a designated location.

4:30   Close

What to Do Next

- ◆ Prepare for the one-day session.

- ◆ Compile the learning activities, handouts, and PowerPoint slides you will use in the training and thoroughly familiarize yourself with their content.

- ◆ Decide whether to offer the advanced issues in strategic planning workshop by reviewing the next chapter.

◆ ◆ ◆

The next chapter includes an agenda and learning activities for a workshop on advanced issues in strategic planning. This workshop builds on the foundation knowledge gleaned from the fundamentals workshop and is targeted at those people who are leading the organization's strategic-planning process.

Slide 6–1

Fundamentals of Strategic Planning

Exploring the foundations of
effectively planning
for the future

Slide 6–2

What ensures the
long-term success
of an organization?

Slide 6–3

The Planning School of
Strategy Formation

Slide 6–4

The Fallacies of Strategic Planning

1. The future is predictable vs. the future is unknowable

2. Strategic planning protects the organization vs. nothing protects/insulates

3. Organizational alignment ensures success vs. strategic control can stifle innovation

4. The plan provides a road map vs. there are no road maps that chart uncertainty

Slide 6–5

The Fallacies, *continued* . . .

5. The plan prepares people to be strategic thinkers when needed vs. strategic planning isn't strategic thinking

6. The leadership team develops strategy vs. strategic thinking and action are everybody's business

7. The strategic plan enables learning and growth vs. learning and growth are nonlinear and serendipitous (that is, maybe it will happen, and maybe it won't!)

Slide 6–6

Organizational Longevity . . .

1. Has compelling vision of what is possible and a core ideology that the organization believes.

2. Is sensitive and adaptive to a changing world.

3. Enables people to feel a sense of community/belonging.

4. Has a driving commitment to new ideas, learning, innovation, and continuous improvement.

5. Has a free-flow of divergent ideas, information, and knowledge.

6. Has a front line with the capacity to act independently.

7. Has reward systems that are fair, equitable, and that reward innovation, risk taking, and quality.

8. Takes a conservative approach to financial and other resources.

Slide 6–7

Our Learning Objectives

- Define strategic planning and describe the common components of a strategic plan.

- Describe the role that strategic planning plays in enabling long-term success.

- Identify how strategic planning differs from other forms of organizational planning.

- Develop strategic-thinking skills in oneself and others.

- Apply the key stages of the strategic-planning process.

- Identify methods for involving stakeholders in strategy formulation and implementation.

- Describe common obstacles to strategic planning and ways to overcome these obstacles.

Slide 6–8

Meet and Greet!

- Introduce yourself to your table partners.

- Share your personal objective(s) for the day.

- As a group, identify some common goals and issues of interest.

- Develop two or three questions about strategic planning and thinking that your group would like to have answered before the end of the day.

Slide 6–9

Perceptions of Strategic Planning

- What is your definition of strategic planning? What does it mean to plan strategically?

- What positives can strategic planning help create for an organization?

- What negatives might it also create (if we're not careful)?

Slide 6–10

Strategic Planning Is . . .

Strateg(os) — the art of the general.

A *systematic* process for making decisions and managing work to guide an organization toward its desired outcomes.

- Making decisions with an awareness of the future and an awareness of the implications of each future-minded decision.

- Organizing systematically the actions of work areas, teams, and individuals to carry out these future-minded decisions.

- Measuring the results of these actions and decisions against expectations.

Slide 6–11

Components of a Strategic Plan . . .

✓ *Vision* — A description of the *ideal* future and the outcomes it hopes to create for its stakeholders

✓ *Mission Statement* — A description of who the organization serves and how the organization will structure itself

✓ *Core Values and Beliefs* — Statements of belief describing behaviors/ideas to guide actions

✓ *Strategic Issues* — Key issues to address to close the gap between the *ideal* and the *real*

✓ *Critical Success Factors* — Broad measures indicating that the organization is making progress toward the vision

✓ *Departmental strategic plans* — The long-range plan each department creates to translate the plan to department action

✓ *Operational/Budgeting Plans* — The decisions/actions that departments, work teams, and individuals will take to implement the strategic agenda

Slide 6–12

Insanity . . .

Repeatedly doing
the same things
in the same way
and expecting
different results.

Slide 6–13

What is the
purpose of a
strategic plan?

13

Slide 6–14

The Purposes of Strategic Planning

- Identify the organization's aspirations and the challenges it will face
- Clarify and gain consensus around strategy
- Communicate this strategy throughout the organization
- Align departmental and personal goals with the overarching organizational strategy
- Identify and align strategic initiatives

14

Slide 6–15

The Purposes, *continued* . . .

- Measure/evaluate progress in achieving its vision and strategy
- Identify opportunities for improvement and learning
- Direct skill- and knowledge-building efforts
- Increase the probability of the organization's ongoing relevance in the marketplace
- Guide decision making by leaders, managers, and staff
- Guide resource allocation and budget planning

15

Slide 6–16

If you don't know where
you're going . . .

any road will get you there.

16

Slide 6–17

Strategic Thinking

Strategic thinking involves . . .

- Holding an image of the vision or ideal future in one's mind
- Drawing on and being shaped by the organization's core values
- Continuously scanning the environment, looking for opportunities and threats
- Seeing the patterns and relationships in events and circumstances
- Recognizing the interconnections and interdependencies before making decisions and taking action
- Making decisions and taking actions for the long-term that are shaped by the vision, core values, awareness of the environment, and awareness of the interdependencies

17

Slide 6–18

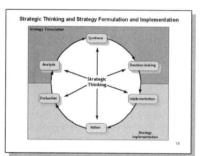

Slide 6–19

Actions to Develop the Strategic-Thinking Mindset

In your small group, answer these questions:

1. What actions can individuals take to develop a strategic-thinking mindset in themselves?
2. What actions can the organization take to develop the strategic-thinking mindset in employees and other stakeholders?

19

Slide 6–20

Developing Strategic Thinkers

- Repeatedly communicate the vision.
- Integrate the vision and core values into individual performance goals and performance reviews.
- Make the vision and core values part of meetings, celebrations, problem analysis and solving, and so forth.
- Invite people to share/discuss what they are learning from their customers and what they see happening around them that might have a bearing on the organization's future success.
- Debrief challenges, problems, and crises from a strategic perspective.

20

Slide 6–21

Planning Levels

Planning Level	Desired Result	Style of Action	Underlying Value	C %	D %
Strategic	Achieve ideal future; optimize outcomes, given resources and constraints	Future-minded; has long-term focus; explores alternative possibilities	Controlled instability and optimization of opportunities	%	%
Interactive	Exceed expectations; anticipate daily problems	Proactive	Continuous improvement	%	%
Operational	Maintain status quo; conform to expectations; control results; turn plans into action	Has short-term focus; fixes problems; maintains smooth operation	Stability and control	%	%
Tactical	Satisfy customer expectations; solve problems	Reactive	Survival and responsiveness	%	%
				100%	100%

Slide 6–22

How Do You Spend YOUR Time?

In your small groups . . .

- Share your "current" and "desired" percentages.
- *Discuss:* Is there an "ideal" distribution of our planning time? What is it?
- *Discuss:* What prevents us from achieving our ideal distribution of our time?
- *Discuss:* What are the consequences for (a) the organization and (b) individuals if we spend most of our time at the tactical/operational levels?

22

Slide 6–23

Planning Levels

Planning Level	Desired Result	Style of Action	Underlying Value	C %	D %
Strategic	Achieve ideal future; optimize outcomes, given resources and constraints	Future-minded; has long-term focus; explores alternative possibilities	Controlled instability and optimization of opportunities	%	%
Interactive	Exceed expectations; anticipate daily problems	Proactive	Continuous improvement	%	%
Operational	Maintain status quo; conform to expectations; control results; turn plans into action	Has short-term focus; fixes problems; maintains smooth operation	Stability and control	%	%
Tactical	Satisfy customer expectations; solve problems	Reactive	Survival and responsiveness	%	%
				100%	100%

Slide 6–24

Escaping from the Tactical

In your small groups . . .

- Identify actions that individuals or organizations can take to enable employees to "escape" from the captivity of the tactical or tactical/operational levels of planning.

24

Slide 6–25

Escaping from the Tactical

- Gather data.
- Gain the "1,000-feet-high" perspective.
- Take a time-out.
- Reflect on the past.
- Focus on common causes.
- Draw on the vision and core values.
- Create new systems and structures.

25

Slide 6–26

It's not enough to be industrious; so are the ants. What are you industrious about?

— Henry David Thoreau
American author/philosopher
(b. 1817 - d. 1862)

26

Slide 6–27

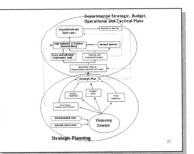

27

Slide 6–28

Destiny is no matter of chance. It is a matter of choice: It is not a thing to be waited for, it is a thing to be achieved.

— William Jennings Bryan
American statesman and politician
(b. 1860 - d. 1925)

28

Slide 6–29

Stages of Developing a Strategic Plan

- Stage 1 ⟶ A. Take stock of the present
  B. Conduct a SWOT analysis

- Stage 2 ⟶ A. Create a shared vision
  B. Define key values/beliefs

- Stage 3 ⟶ A. Identify critical issues
  B. Develop goals and plans

- Stage 4 ⟶ A. Develop operational plans
  B. Monitor, evaluate, and revise

29

Slide 6–30

Identify Actions for Each Stage

In your small groups . . .

- Review the "key actions" and questions in the left-hand column for your assigned stage.
- In the right-hand column, identify the specific tools, methods, techniques, and approaches your group would recommend to a strategic-planning team to satisfy the key actions and answer the questions in the left-hand column.

30

Slide 6–31

Stage 1 Actions

- Gather performance *data*.
- Identify *statutes* and *laws* that affect the organization.
- Define the *current* mission and goals.
- Assess how *successful* the organization has been in achieving its mission and goals.
- Using focus groups, surveys, and interviews, gather data from employees, customers, and other stakeholders on their *perceptions of the organization*.
- Assess the *external forces* influencing the organization's future.

31

Slide 6–32

Stage 2 Actions

- Ask people what the organization should *aspire* to accomplish or create for customers, the community, and so forth.
- Explore people's expectations of the *core values* that should govern the way employees work together, make decisions, serve customers, and the like.
- Conduct *focus groups, interviews,* and *surveys* to gather data on expectations, aspirations, hopes, and core values.
- Gather information from people at *all levels* (inside and outside).
- Create a truly *shared vision* by inviting people to contribute their ideas and to make it theirs.

32

Slide 6–33

Stage 3 Actions

- Ask people to *identify the issues* (from SWOT) that are most likely to influence the organization's future.
- *Clarify* each area for action: Do we know what is the goal of addressing an issue? How critical to the organization is achieving this goal?
- Involve people in *prioritizing the issues* from greatest to least impact on the vision.
- For each strategic issue, develop a *detailed action plan* that spells out the goals/outcomes, measures of performance, key actions, who will take action, and the timeline for moving forward.

33

Slide 6–34

Stage 4 Actions

- Each department develops an *operational plan* that helps move the organization toward the vision. Each goal/objective should relate to one of the key organization-wide strategic objectives.
- When issues at the organizational level are specific to a *department* or work area, that department or area takes the lead.
- Initiate *collaborative efforts* (across departmental boundaries) to achieve synergy and avoid duplication and the silo effect.
- Develop a *reporting/communication process* to keep all players involved, responsible, accountable, and informed.
- Develop *semiannual "checks"* on progress, assessing results against the vision, critical success factors, and individual goal measures.
- Ensure accountability by building measurement and progress reports on the plan into the routine business processes of individual departments.
- *Make adjustments* to the plan as it unfolds.

34

Slide 6–35

Who should be involved in developing organizational strategy?

35

Slide 6–36

How Do We Involve Others?

- Which *five* individuals or groups are most important for including in the development of the strategic plan?
- *How* should we involve them? Identify two or three specific ways to include these groups in the planning process.
- How might the planning process be adjusted to accommodate the involvement of each group?

36

Slide 6–37

Quality is impossible if people are afraid to tell the truth.

– W. Edwards Deming
Father of the Quality Improvement movement
(b. 1900 - d. 1993)

37

Slide 6–38

Exploring the Organization's Strategic-Planning Strengths

In your small groups . . .

Identify the organization's competencies and strengths that will enable it to successfully develop and implement a meaningful strategic plan. Consider such questions as these:

– *What has it done well in the past that demonstrates its likely competence at strategic planning?*

– *What does it currently do well that has prepared it for strategic planning?*

38

Slide 6–39

Barriers to Implementation

1. The strategic plan reflects the sometimes abstract world of planners, CEOs, and organizational thinkers.

2. The vision and strategy aren't actionable.

3. Strategy isn't linked to department, unit, team, or individual goals.

4. Organizational strategy isn't usually linked to the organization's system for allocating resources.

5. Performance feedback systems are usually *tactical* rather than *strategic*.

6. The plan fails to anticipate and respond to both incremental and radical change (unplanned events) occurring within and outside of the organization.

39

Slide 6–40

Addressing the Obstacles

In your small groups . . .

■ Identify the most likely obstacles to development and implementation of the strategic plan.

■ Identify organizational strengths and capacities that will enable the organization to overcome these obstacles.

40

Slide 6–41

Summary Thoughts

• Strategic planning plays an essential role by clarifying what's important and focusing organizational efforts.

• Developing strategic thinking at all levels of the organization is just as important as having a strategic plan.

• The tactical and operational levels of planning tend to dominate our daily work because they both stare us in the face.

• There are different approaches to strategic planning and a plan may take different forms.

• Participation helps ensure that the plan reflects the realities at the tactical level, is imbued with the ideas of more than just the leadership, and is accepted by those who must implement it.

41

Slide 6–42

Thank You!

• The next part . . . the hard part . . . is up to you: translating the planning process into something meaningful and real.

• Best of luck in moving forward in your role within the strategic-planning process!

42

One-Day Workshop: Advanced Issues in Strategic Planning

What's in This Chapter?

- List of objectives for the one-day workshop on advanced issues in strategic planning

- Lists of materials for instructor and participants

- Detailed instructions on workshop preparation

- Workshop agenda and facilitator's guide

This chapter presents a workshop that moves beyond the fundamentals offered in chapter 6 by focusing on the more advanced skills and knowledge that will be needed to develop a strategic plan and make it operational. The advanced issues workshop builds on the fundamentals and engages participants in using specific strategic-planning tools and methods.

You will find that this workshop offers practical tools, methods, and approaches for enabling your participants to begin developing a strategic plan. Although the fundamentals workshop presented a broad overview of what a plan is, what it's made of, and the steps for creating a plan, this workshop engages participants in exploring the deeper issues involved in developing a plan and ensuring that it stays relevant beyond the point of its creation.

So, let's get started with our advanced issues workshop, titled Creating the Future: Mastering Strategic-Planning Skills.

Objectives

As a result of participating in this workshop, participants will be able to

- recognize the difference between strategy formulation and strategy implementation

- develop a shared vision for their organization

- identify the core values or guiding principles that support the shared vision and accomplish the strategic agenda

- conduct a SWOT analysis that provides a better understanding of the organization's internal and external environments

- select the key strategic issues that become the organization's strategic agenda

- develop action plans that move the organization toward its vision and mission

- deal effectively with emergent issues and an unknowable future.

Materials

For the instructor:

- Projector, screen, and computer for running the PowerPoint slides

- PowerPoint slides 7–1 through 7–28

- Learning Activity 11–11: Characteristics of an Inspiring Vision for the Future

- Learning Activity 11–12: Creating a Shared Vision for the Future

- Learning Activity 11–13: Defining Core Values

- Learning Activity 11–14: Conducting a SWOT Analysis

- Learning Activity 11–15: Defining the Strategic Agenda

- Learning Activity 11–16: Developing Strategic Action Plans

- Learning Activity 11–17: Implementing the Strategic Plan in the Face of Uncertainty and Chaos

- Tool 12–1: Training Room Configuration and Layout

- Tool 12–4: Workshop Level 1 Evaluation

- Tool 12–5: The Parking Lot

- Tool 12–6: Selecting Group Leaders

- Flipcharts, easels, and marking pens (enough for each small group)

For the participants:

- Tool 12–3: Ah-Ha! Sheet

- Handouts and training instruments needed in the learning activities

Using the CD

Materials for this training session are provided either in this workbook or as electronic files on the accompanying CD. To access the electronic files, insert the CD and click on the appropriate Adobe .pdf document or PowerPoint .ppt/.pps file. Further directions and help using the files can be found in the appendix, "Using the Compact Disc," at the back of this workbook. Thumbnail versions of the PowerPoint slides for this workshop (*Advanced.ppt/.pps*) are included at the end of this chapter.

Preparation

Several months before the workshop:

1. If appropriate, meet with representatives of the executive leadership team to discuss their expectations for this workshop.

2. Review with the executive leadership team the process that will be used for approving, integrating, coordinating, monitoring, and updating the strategic plan. Get the team's agreement on the process you will introduce and describe in the workshop.

3. Schedule the session and arrange for a training room. Ensure that the room has floor space for extensive table-group activity with flipchart easels next to each table. There should be ample wall space to post four large wallcharts (each chart 4 x 6 feet in size and placed at least 6 feet apart).

4. Given the intensive action-oriented aspects of this workshop and the need for both small-group work and large-group integration, limit the number of participants to 24 (ideally, four groups of six people). If you want a larger group, some accommodations will need to be made in the design of the workshop—particularly for Learning Ac-

tivity 11–14: Conducting the SWOT Analysis. See Tool 12–1 for some tips for training room layout.

5. Design the program around the organization's proposed strategic-planning process. Make sure that your training reflects the priorities, focus, and basic approach or methodology of the CEO and the executive leaders or the strategic-planning group.

6. Prepare training materials and familiarize yourself with their content and use.

7. Send an invitation memo, letter, or e-mail to participants, reiterating the purpose of the workshop and its importance in developing the organization's strategic plan. It may be helpful to have this communication come from your CEO or chief operations officer to reinforce the significance and value of program participation.

8. Order food and beverages as necessary.

Just prior to the workshop:

1. Arrive early at the training room.

2. Check room setup and make needed adjustments.

3. Set out flipcharts and markers, and test equipment such as LCD and overhead projectors. Be sure to position the easels so they don't impede anyone's line of sight.

4. Prepare the four 4 x 6-foot wallcharts around the room, labeling each with their respective SWOT titles (see Learning Activity 11–14). Use butcher paper, newsprint, or several flipchart pages taped together to create these posters.

5. Prepare and post a flipchart page titled "Parking Lot" (Tool 12–5), if desired, and any additional flipchart pages called for in the learning activities. You may also want to post another flipchart page highlighting key objective-related questions to be addressed during the workshop.

6. Display PowerPoint slide 7–1 as a welcome to participants and greet them individually as they enter the room.

Sample Agenda

8:30 a.m.   Welcome (5 minutes)

Welcome participants to the Advanced Issues Workshop. Introduce yourself, and display slide 7–2 as you highlight the day's learning objectives. Emphasize that this session is action oriented and that everyone will have an opportunity to practice a number of tools and methods as well as to learn practical tips for developing a strategic plan.

8:35   Questions on advanced issues in strategic planning (20 minutes)

First ask participants to choose table group leaders, using any of the ideas described in Tool 12–6.

Ask participants to reflect on the Fundamentals workshop. Display slide 7–3 and instruct groups to identify two or three questions that they have about strategic planning as they have learned it so far or about the practical aspects of developing and implementing a strategic plan. Give them five minutes to identify their questions.

Reconvene the large group and ask each small group to report one of its questions. Record the questions on a flipchart. Work in a round-robin fashion through all groups until all key questions are identified and recorded.

Post the flipchart pages so everyone can see them. Explain that this advanced issues workshop is intended to be practical in helping them develop a strategic plan, so they and you should focus on finding answers to these questions. Encourage participants to call out specific questions at times when it seems appropriate to address those questions, and thereby to take the lead in finding answers. Make a promise to the group that you will do the same.

Distribute Tool 12–3. Encourage them to be active participants in their own learning by using the Ah-Ha! Sheet to record key learning moments and the insights that will be most useful to them beyond today's session.

Note the schedule for breaks and lunch and the locations of restrooms, telephones, and refreshments.

8:55 Learning Activity 11–11: Characteristics of an Inspiring Vision for the Future (25 minutes)

Vision is key to every strategic plan. It is the place of departure; it defines what the organization hopes to create or accomplish over (and even beyond) the life of the plan. This activity introduces the role and importance of creating a *shared* vision, highlights the core elements that strengthen the vision, and provides some examples for the group.

Option: If the organization has a current vision statement, participants can react to the statement in the later part of the activity.

9:20 Learning Activity 11–12: Creating a Shared Vision for the Future (60 minutes)

This is a highly interactive and energizing activity in which participants will learn one method for developing the vision statement. Side benefits include the creation of various vision statements by the diverse groups and a summary of key vision themes—all of which can be used by the organization as part of the strategic-planning process.

Just before you interrupt this activity with a break, announce that groups will be asked to report their vision statements when they return.

10:00 Break (15 minutes)

10:15 Learning Activity 11–12, continued

Ask each group leader to report his or her group's vision statement. Make note of any themes that emerge across the groups.

10:35 Learning Activity 11–13: Defining Core Values (35 minutes)

This activity highlights the importance of core values in shaping the daily work of people at all levels of the organization. Participants will learn a methodology for identifying core values, which they can then apply throughout the organization.

11:10   Learning Activity 11–14: Conducting a SWOT Analysis (50 minutes)

In this activity, participants conduct a SWOT (strengths, weaknesses, opportunities, threats) analysis for the organization. They learn the importance of the SWOT to strategic planning and thinking and develop a list of strategic issues that can be used within a planning process.

Noon   Lunch (60 minutes)

1:00 p.m.   Learning Activity 11–15: Defining the Strategic Agenda (45 minutes)

Choosing the specific strategies that the organization must pursue if it is to realize its vision is a key step (Phase 3) in the strategic-planning process. This activity offers participants insights into how to define the strategic agenda and presents a process for selecting the "high-leverage" strategies. Participants also learn about the "balanced scorecard"—an approach to developing the strategic agenda that emphasizes the value of pursuing multiple reinforcing strategic goals (rather than pursuing only one, such as profits).

The organization can use the results from this process of selecting a strategic agenda in its planning process.

1:45   Learning Activity 11–16: Developing Strategic Action Plans (25 minutes)

At some point every planning process moves from *strategy formulation* (the first phases of the process) to *strategy implementation*—where the action plan becomes operational within the organization. This activity introduces a template for action planning that participants can use to develop the formal step-by-step process of translating the plan into actions and accountabilities.

2:10   Break (15 minutes)

2:25   Approving, coordinating, integrating, and updating the strategic plan (35 minutes)

Suggest to the participants that finalizing, coordinating, monitoring, and updating the plan are usually the responsibilities of the organization's executive leadership team. Indicate that this group receives the proposed/recommended strategic agenda action plans at the organizational and subunit levels and gives its final approval to commit organizational resources to implementation. Note that this team also plays a key role in helping the organization respond to a changing environment by altering strategy or direction and updating or revising the plan when needed.

Distribute any documentation that you and organizational leaders have developed that explains the structure created for coordinating, integrating, monitoring, and updating the plan.

Ask participants to work in groups to review the proposed process for approving, integrating, coordinating, monitoring, and updating or revising the plan. Ask each group to select a leader (using a method from Training Tool 12–6) to guide the group in identifying questions they may have about this process. Give the groups 10 minutes to review, discuss, and identify their questions.

Reconvene the large group and ask for general questions about the approval, integration, coordination, monitoring, and revision process. Encourage people to offer their ideas for answers/solutions to questions posed. Record any unanswered questions on the Parking Lot flipchart page for future consideration by the executive leadership team or for follow-up with the participants.

3:00   Learning Activity 11–17: Implementing the Strategic Plan in the Face of Uncertainty and Chaos (45 minutes)

Make a transition from the previous activity by noting that a plan must be responsive to changes in the environment if it is to remain relevant.

This activity links to the opening discussion in the Fundamentals of Strategic Planning and Thinking Workshop by highlighting the challenge of sustaining strategic thinking and planning in the face of daily operations and especially during times of tumultuous change. Participants explore the effects of emergent issues and an unknowable future on a strategic plan and develop some methods for ensuring the plan's responsiveness.

3:45   Review, integration, and question review (40 minutes)

Bring the workshop to a close by referring to the questions that the group asked at the beginning of the day. Check off those questions that the workshop has directly addressed and identify those that may remain unanswered. Assign each of the unanswered questions to one or more of the groups and ask them to spend the next 10 minutes developing a response. Invite them to draw together the methods and tools they discussed and practiced today to help them create the response. If a group's assigned question requires an executive team response, encourage the group to develop the response that they would like to hear from that team or one that reflects what the group believes to be the best practice. Ask each group to select a new small-group leader to guide the discussion.

Reconvene the group and use the remaining time to guide the large group in sharing answers to the questions. If there are any unanswered questions remaining, explain that they will be forwarded to the executive leadership team for a response.

4:25   Evaluation (5 minutes)

Display slide 7–28. Thank the participants for attending the workshop and for their active involvement throughout the session. Distribute the evaluation form (Tool 12–4) and encourage participants to leave their completed forms at their tables or at a designated location.

4:30   Close

What to Do Next

- Prepare for the one-day session on Advanced Issues in Strategic Planning.

- Customize the materials you will use in the workshop to ensure that they reflect the organization's actual practice and expectations for its strategic planning.

- Compile the learning activities, handouts, training instruments, tools, and PowerPoint slides you will use in the training and thoroughly familiarize yourself with their content.

- Decide whether to offer the half-day workshop on developing strategic thinking by reviewing the next chapter.

◆ ◆ ◆

The next chapter presents a half-day workshop on developing strategic thinkers at every level of the organization. Those people who participated in the Advanced Issues workshop would also benefit from this program that more deeply explores ways to strengthen strategic thinking throughout the organization.

Slide 7–1

Advanced Issues in Strategic Planning and Thinking

Creating the Future:
Mastering Strategic-Planning
and Strategic-Thinking Skills

Slide 7–2

Learning Objectives

- Recognize the difference between strategy formulation and strategy implementation
- Identify methods for developing a shared vision
- Identify the core values or guiding principles that support the shared vision and accomplish the strategic agenda
- Conduct a SWOT analysis that enables a better understanding of the organization's internal and external environments
- Select the key strategic issues that become the organization's strategic agenda
- Develop action plans that move the organization toward the vision/mission
- Deal effectively with emergent issues and an unknowable future

Slide 7–3

Your Questions/Issues

In your small groups . . .

- Discuss your personal objectives for today's workshop.
- Based on the personal objectives discussions, identify two or three specific questions or issues that your group would like to have addressed during the workshop—particularly questions or issues around strategic-plan development and implementation.

Slide 7–4

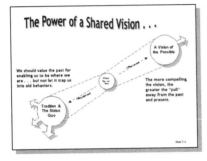

The Power of a Shared Vision . . .

Slide 7–5

Characteristics of an Inspiring Vision

- What makes a vision inspiring?
- What characteristics enable a vision to captivate the hopes and aspirations of the human spirit?

Slide 7–6

An Inspiring Vision . . .

- Captures people's imagination concerning what is possible
- Engages people's spirit/passion
- Inspires people to excellence
- Provides a clear and compelling alternative to the present
- Taps into people's innate human desire for hope and higher aspirations
- Provides a standard or benchmark for evaluating or assessing the quality of their actions
- Challenges people to unite and focus their energies toward a common goal/good

Slide 7–7

Sample Vision Statements

1. Which vision statements capture *your* imagination?
2. Which vision statements paint a vivid picture of the world as they want it to be?
3. What makes some of these vision statements work for you?

Slide 7–8

Sharing Your Aspirations

In your small group . . .
- Share your postcard images and impressions.
- Based on your collective postcard aspirations, develop a flipchart page that highlights the key themes that emerge from your stories:
  - What images do you have in common?
  - What is the collective story that emerges from your individual stories?
- Use colored markers, pictures, graphics—anything that helps you communicate the shared ideas and themes from your team's postcard stories.
- Be prepared to share your vision themes with the large group. Use poetry, song, rap, a story, a fairy tale, and so forth. Have fun promoting your vision of the future!

Slide 7–9

Characteristics of Core Values

- Tap into the existing belief structure of those who choose to work for the organization
- Speak to what is right, moral, and has the highest integrity.
- Enable individuals to identify how the core values directly influence their work, decision making, and so forth.
- Move beyond the self-interest of the organization
- Enable stakeholders to make independent decisions
- Enable individuals to assess their own decisions and actions
- Enable the CEO/COO, BoD, and leadership team to make decisions and take actions within a framework in concert with the vision and strategic agenda
- Are stated in the *present* tense

Slide 7–10

Sample Core Values

- Diverse opinions and discussions enhance our decision making and contribute to our success.
- Our leaders are responsive, visible, and supportive to all members of the organization.
- Partnerships enhance the effectiveness of our team.
- The quality of what we do is measured by the satisfaction of those we serve.
- We put ethics above profits.
- We continually improve the way we do business and we are responsive to the need to change.

Slide 7–11

Core Values Exercise

- Working by yourself, complete Training Instrument 11-13.
- Take the next 10 minutes to work through each of the steps of the exercise. It is important not to move too quickly and not to skip a step.

Slide 7–12

Sharing and Discussing Your Core Values

- Individually, share the top three core values that guide your daily work and life.
- As a group, develop a list of the core values most frequently being mentioned, and then settle on the top four or five core values that emerge from the group.

Slide 7–13

The Forces We Face

As you reflect on the environment within which this organization operates, what are the two or three most significant forces that are likely to shape the organization's future success?

Slide 7–14

The SWOT Analysis

Internal
- **Strengths** — what we do well
- **Weaknesses** — where we need to improve

External
- **Opportunities** — trends and events outside of the organization of which we can take advantage
- **Threats** — trends and events outside the organization that could jeopardize the organization's success

Slide 7–15

Internal: Organizational Strengths

Reflecting on this organization's *internal* capacities, systems, methods, processes . . .

- What does this organization do well?
- What do you feel proud of here?
- What represents the "rock" on which the organization will achieve its vision?
- What capacities/abilities are likely to enable the organization's success over the long term?

Slide 7–16

Internal: Areas for Improvement

Reflecting on this organization's *internal* capacities, systems, methods, processes . . .

- What doesn't this organization do well?
- In which areas does the organization fail you or its customers?
- What aspects of the organization represent a vulnerability that could jeopardize its future success?
- What capacities/abilities are likely to significantly erode the organization's success?
- What frustrates you about how the organization operates or functions?

Slide 7–17

External: Opportunities

Reflecting on the *external* environment within which the organization operates . . .

- What trends or events are occurring outside the organization that are likely to have a significant and positive effect on its future success?
- What external trends could benefit the organization if it found a way to "ride the wave" of the opportunity into a successful future?

Slide 7–18

External: Threats

Reflecting on the *external* environment within which the organization operates . . .

- What trends or events are occurring outside the organization that are likely to have a significant negative effect on the organization's future success?
- What external trends could jeopardize the organization's future success if they were ignored or not addressed by the organization?

Slide 7–19

Identifying the Strategic Agenda

As you consider various approaches for defining the strategic agenda, keep the following questions in mind:

- Which approach for selecting the strategic agenda seems most appropriate for the organization?
- What isn't clear about any of these approaches to selecting the strategic agenda?

Slide 7–20

Selecting the Strategic Agenda

In your small group . . .

- Discuss the different approaches to selecting the strategic agenda.
- Strive for consensus on which approach would be most useful for the organization.
- Discuss and seek to clarify any of the methods that were confusing or unclear.

Slide 7–21

High Leverage . . .

Specific actions whereby a small, well-focused effort produces the most significant and *enduring* improvements or changes

Slide 7–22

Action-Planning Template

- What is the strategic issue?
- What sustains or causes this issue?
- What will the outcome look like? What is the end result of addressing this issue?
- What is the two- to three-year strategic goal for the issue?
- What are obstacles to the goal?
- What are some ideas for achieving the strategic goal?
- What are the final actions and accountabilities?
- What are the resources required and their sources?

Slide 7–23

Reactions to the Action-Planning Template

1. What do you like about the action plan template?
2. What isn't clear about the template or how it would be used?
3. What questions do you have about the template and its use?
4. How might you improve the template to better meet the organization's needs or approach to strategic planning?

Slide 7–24

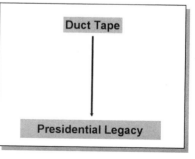

Duct Tape

↓

Presidential Legacy

Slide 7–25

Chaos and Complexity

- There is a natural, implicit order or structure to all living things.
- Organizations are living systems that learn, grow, react, initiate actions, and so forth.
- This natural order is not always apparent or evident—and then typically only at a distance and over time.
- You cannot impose order on or control a living system; all you can do is influence its actions and future.

Slide 7–26

Chaos Theory and Strategic Planning . . .

On your own . . .

1. What are the implications of these theories for strategic planning? How do they affect how the organization develops, implements, and sustains the strategic plan?

2. Which "principle" of chaos and complexity theories is most significant in its impact on strategic planning? Why?

Slide 7–27

Chaos Theory and Strategic Planning . . .

In your small group . . .

- Discuss the implications of these theories for strategic planning and how they affect the way the organization develops, implements, and sustains the strategic plan.
- Discuss which "principle" of chaos and complexity theories is most significant in its impact on strategic planning.
- Identify specific actions that *individuals* can take to integrate the lessons from chaos and complexity theories into the strategic-planning process. [Record on flipchart]
- Identify specific actions that the *organization* can take to ensure that the lessons from chaos and complexity theories are integrated into the strategic planning process. [Record on flipchart]

Slide 7–28

Thank You!

- You are encouraged to take the tools, methods, approaches, and insights from today's session and begin integrating them into your daily *strategic* practice—and your planning processes.
- Continue your efforts to keep the emerging strategic plan alive and relevant—ensuring that it focuses on the right strategic agenda to guide the organization successfully into the future.
- And . . . keep your eyes open for those "duct tape" events that could change the course of the organization.

Chapter 8

Half-Day Workshop: Developing Strategic Thinkers

What's in This Chapter?

- List of objectives for the half-day workshop on developing strategic thinkers

- Lists of materials for instructor and participants

- Detailed instructions on workshop preparation

- Workshop agenda and facilitator's guide

As this book has argued from the beginning, strategic thinking and planning must be everyone's responsibility—staff on the front line as well as those in the boardroom. In fact, without strategic thinkers throughout the organization and at every level, key insights will be lost and the strategies the organization pursues will likely be flawed. This chapter strives to address the issue by presenting a workshop that develops both strategic thinkers and the skills of strategic thinking.

This half-day workshop is a hands-on session that deeply engages participants in thinking strategically about their organization, the environment within which it operates, the strategies that it has embraced, and their individual roles within the organization. For this reason, leading this workshop involves more facilitating a process that engages people in strategic thinking than simply building skills.

Beyond developing the competencies of strategic thinking in those who participate, a side benefit of this workshop is generating a set of ideas and issues that can be used in developing a strategic plan or in updating or revising the current plan. As you prepare to offer this workshop, decide on both your target audience and how the results will be used with the current or emerging strategic plan. We encourage you to offer the workshop as a cascading series of seminars that touch all of the organization and that gather useful and actionable strategic insights from all levels. The results will be employees throughout the organization who begin to think and act strategically and a stream of useful strategic insights that can inform the current strategic plan or help focus the development of a new plan.

Objectives

As a result of participating in this workshop, participants will be able to

- describe the role that strategic thinking plays in the long-term success of an organization

- identify the competencies needed for strategic thinking

- develop a mindmap that identifies key strategic issues that face the organization today and are likely to affect it in the future

- develop a personal plan for adjusting current and future decisions and behaviors to those of a strategic thinker.

Materials

For the instructor:

- Projector, screen, and computer for running the PowerPoint slides

- PowerPoint slides 8–1 through 8–10

- Learning Activity 11–5: Value of Strategic Thinking

- Learning Activity 11–18: Developing the Strategic Issues Map

- Tool 12–1: Training Room Configuration and Layout

- Tool 12–4: Workshop Level 1 Evaluation

- Flipchart, easel, and marking pens

- Whiteboard or paper, 4 x 12 feet, and appropriate markers. The larger the writing space, the better; but this activity can be done on smaller work surfaces. Use newsprint or butcher paper, or tape together several sheets of flipchart paper.

For the participants:

- Handouts and training instruments needed in the learning activities

- Tool 12–3: Ah-Ha! Sheet

Using the CD

Materials for this training session are provided either in this workbook or as electronic files on the accompanying CD. To access the electronic files, insert the CD and click on the appropriate Adobe .pdf document or PowerPoint .ppt/.pps file. Further directions and help using the files can be found in the appendix, "Using the Compact Disc," at the back of this workbook. Thumbnail versions of the PowerPoint slides for this workshop (*Strategic Thinkers.ppt/.pps*) are included at the end of this chapter.

Preparation

Several months before the workshop:

1. Meet with a representative or representatives from the executive leadership team or the group charged with developing or revising the strategic plan to discuss how they will use and integrate the results of this workshop into the current or emerging strategic plan. Ensure that this group has a chance to identify specific issues or questions they would like participants to explore during the session.

2. Identify your target audience. This workshop builds critical strategic thinking skills in frontline staff and managers and is, therefore, geared to all audiences. Because the key objective is to engage as many organizational stakeholders in the process of strategic thinking as possible, we strongly recommend that all employees participate. Create mixed groups of participants, including frontline staff and middle- and upper-level managers. Diversity is important here to strengthen the degree of strategic thinking at *every* organizational level. If you mix various organizational levels in this workshop, participants are more likely to hear, interact with, and learn from each other—particularly in relation to the strategic issues facing the organization.

   Note: Although it is possible to facilitate a larger group, the maximum benefit is gained from groups of 15 to 25 people.

   The workshop can be offered as a stand-alone workshop that simply engages organizational stakeholders in strategic thinking or it can be offered as a follow-on workshop to the one-day fundamentals or advanced issues workshops.

3. Schedule the session and arrange for a training room. Ensure that the room has ample wall space for the large whiteboard or paper on

which participants can map the strategic issues they see influencing the organization today and in the near future. See Tool 12–1 for help with the ideal room layout.

4. Discuss with the organization's leaders the value of integrating the strategic issues identified in this workshop into the emerging strategic plan. Confirming that the workshop results will be used beyond the workshop tends to increase the level of participation and the quality of the work.

5. Prepare training materials and familiarize yourself with their content and operation.

6. Send an invitation memo, letter, or e-mail to participants, reiterating the purpose of the workshop and its importance in developing or adjusting the organization's strategic plan. Emphasize the value of strategic thinkers to the organization's long-term success, both in plan design and in employees' daily decisions and actions. It may be helpful to have this communication come from your CEO or chief operations officer to reinforce the significance and value of program participation.

7. Order refreshments as necessary.

Just prior to the workshop:

1. Arrive early at the training room.

2. Check room setup and make needed adjustments. Ensure that there is enough space for both small and large groups to work near a large wall poster or whiteboard to create the strategic issues mindmap.

3. Set out flipcharts and markers, and test equipment such as LCD and overhead projectors.

4. Prepare and hang the wallchart or whiteboard that is to be used for the strategic issues mindmap exercise. Prepare any additional flipchart pages as detailed in the learning activities. You may also want to post another flipchart page highlighting key objective-related questions to be addressed during the workshop.

5. Display PowerPoint slide 8–1 as a welcome to participants and greet them individually as they enter the room.

Sample Agenda

8:30 a.m.   Welcome (5 minutes)

Welcome participants to the Developing Strategic Thinkers Workshop. Introduce yourself and highlight the learning objectives of the workshop. Point out the dual focus for this workshop: (1) developing the competencies of strategic thinking and (2) identifying a set of current and emerging strategic issues that should be integrated into the current or developing strategic plan.

Display slide 8–2. Indicate that a key outcome from the workshop will be a list of strategic issues identified by the group that the executive leadership team or strategic-planning steering committee will use in developing or updating the organization's strategic plan.

If this workshop follows either the fundamentals or advanced workshop on strategic planning, note the relationship between those workshops and this one. Make the point that whereas these other workshops were focused on developing an understanding of the strategic-planning process, this workshop focuses on developing skills that enable employees to make daily decisions and take actions within a larger strategic focus.

Distribute Tool 12–3. Encourage participants to be active in their own learning by using the Ah-Ha! Sheet to record key learning moments and the insights that will be most useful to them beyond today's session.

Note the schedule for breaks and the location of restrooms, telephones, and refreshments.

8:35   Learning Activity 11–5: Value of Strategic Thinking (35 minutes)

This activity develops insights into the role of strategic thinking in good planning and organizational success.

Explain that a strategic plan is important to the long-term success of an organization because it helps stakeholders at every level make decisions and take action within a strategic context—and that developing strategic thinkers is just as important. Point out that a strategic plan is only relevant to the extent that it benefits from the daily insights and emergent issues that surface from the organization's tactical and operational levels, and so strategic thinkers are needed at these levels.

For some participants this may be a review; for others, the idea of "strategic thinking" will be a new concept. Your primary goal here is to emphasize the role that strategic thinking plays in daily decision making and action rather than to emphasize the creation of a strategic plan.

Note: If all of the participants attending this session attended the Fundamentals workshop, much of this learning activity can be abbreviated (for example, by eliminating the steps for developing the personal plan). At a minimum, however, this activity should remind participants of the importance of strategic thinking to the health, vitality, and long-term success of the organization.

9:10   Learning Activity 11–18: Developing the Strategic Issues Map (130 minutes)

Transition the group from the concepts of strategic planning and thinking to a principle underlying both: the importance of understanding the current environment and being able to identify issues, behaviors, trends, incidents, and so forth that are likely to have a direct or indirect bearing on the organization today, tomorrow, or even several years from now.

This exercise requires people to move around, write on the wallchart or whiteboard, and discuss in small groups the implications of the strategic issues mindmap.

10:00   Break (15 minutes)

Note: Break at some point in the mindmapping process—typically before you guide the small groups into identifying the implications of the map.

10:15   Learning Activity 11–18, continued

The second portion of the mindmapping process has you reconvening small groups to identify and discuss the implications of the mindmap for the organization as a whole and for their personal daily decisions and actions.

The last segment of this activity involves participants in completing a personal plan that identifies how they will use the insights gained in the workshop in their daily decisions and actions.

11:35   Integration (20 minutes)

Summarize the key findings from the strategic issues mapping process and note that these issues will be compiled and forwarded to those who are developing or revising the strategic plan. Emphasize, however, that the main point of today's workshop was less about shaping the strategic plan than it was about shaping how each of them thinks about their own daily decisions and behaviors within a strategic context.

11:55   Evaluation (5 minutes)

Display slide 8–10. Thank the participants for attending the workshop and for their active involvement throughout the session. Distribute Tool 12–4 and encourage participants to leave their completed evaluations at their tables or at a designated location.

Noon   Close

What to Do Next

◆ Prepare for the half-day session on developing strategic thinkers.

◆ Customize the learning activities and materials you will use in the workshop to ensure that they reflect the organization's actual practice and plans for strategic planning.

◆ Compile the learning activities, handouts, training instruments, tools, and PowerPoint slides you will use in the training and thoroughly familiarize yourself with their content.

◆ Ensure you have the space to create the Strategic Issues Map using a large wallchart or whiteboard, and that both small groups and the full class can be arranged to face the wall with the map on it.

◆ Develop a process for transcribing the strategic issues maps from all of the Developing Strategic Thinkers workshops and for making them available to the group that is leading the development or revision of the strategic plan.

◆◆◆

The next two chapters present one-day workshops on problem solving and decision making (PSDM) within a strategic framework. The principles of PSDM will be presented as will models to guide the PSDM process. An array of tools will be introduced and practiced to enable participants to address issues at the tactical, operational, and strategic levels effectively.

Slide 8–1

Developing Strategic Thinkers

Strengthening Strategic Thinking at
All Organizational Levels

Slide 8–2

Learning Objectives

- Describe the role that strategic thinking plays in the long-term success of an organization
- Identify the competencies of strategic thinking
- Develop a strategic issues mindmap that identifies key strategic issues facing the organization today and likely to affect it in the future
- Develop a personal plan for adjusting current and future decisions and behavior to reflect the results of becoming more of a strategic thinker

Slide 8–3

Strategic Thinking

Strategic thinking involves . . .

- Holding an image of the vision or ideal future in one's mind
- Drawing on and being shaped by the organization's core values
- Continuously scanning the environment, looking for opportunities and threats
- Seeing the patterns and relationships in events and circumstances
- Recognizing the interconnections and interdependencies before making decisions and taking action
- Making decisions and taking actions for the long term that are shaped by the vision, core values, awareness of the environment, and awareness of the interdependencies

Slide 8–4

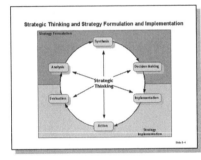

Strategic Thinking and Strategy Formulation and Implementation

Slide 8–5

Actions to Develop the Strategic-Thinking Mindset

In your small group, identify . . .

- What actions can individuals take to develop a strategic-thinking mindset in themselves?
- What actions can the organization take to develop the strategic-thinking mindset in employees and other stakeholders?

Slide 8–6

Developing Strategic Thinkers

- Repeatedly communicate the vision.
- Integrate the vision and core values into individual performance goals and performance reviews.
- Make the vision and core values part of meetings, celebrations, problem analysis and solving, and so forth.
- Invite people to share/discuss what they are learning from their customers and what they see happening around them that might have a bearing on the organization's future success.
- Debrief challenges, problems, and crises from a strategic perspective.

Slide 8–7

Why is strategic __thinking__ more important than strategic planning?

Slide 8–8

Implications and Actions

1. What are the implications for operational and strategic planning as suggested by the Strategic Issues Map?
2. What actions should individuals take in response to the Strategic Issues Map?
3. What actions should the organization take in response to the Strategic Issues Map?

Slide 8–9

Developing Your Personal Plan

Working by yourself . . .

- Identify some specific actions you can take that reflect insights from the Strategic Issues Map . . .
  - Personal actions that reflect strategic thinking
  - Personal actions that reflect your role as a strategic thinker at the operational, tactical, and strategic levels of planning

Slide 8–10

Thank You!

- Ensure that you integrate the insights from the Strategic Issues Map into your daily thoughts and actions.
- Move forward with your personal plan.
- Continue to reflect on the Strategic Issues Map and its implications for the organization, your team, and your own role in the organization.
- Sustain your strategic-thinking skills.

One-Day Workshop: Strategic Problem Solving and Decision Making

What's in This Chapter?

- List of objectives for the one-day workshop on strategic PSDM
- Lists of materials for instructor and participants
- Detailed instructions on workshop preparation
- Workshop agenda and facilitator's guide

A strategic plan provides operational guidance to people at every level of the organization. When effective, the strategic plan and its components—such as the vision, core values, and strategic issues—help employees make decisions and solve problems in ways that support the overarching purpose of the organization while responding to the presenting problem or accomplishing the goal.

The methods that people use to make decisions and solve problems should be deeply connected to and informed by the organization's vision, the core values, and strategic issues. Furthermore, as we discussed in chapter 2, complex learning is essential to strategic thinking and planning. So also is the integration of the wisdom, the insight, and the foresight that emerge from the interaction and deliberative dialogue among diverse stakeholders. It is within this strategic context and in pursuit of both learning and the integration of diverse perspectives that we offer a one-day workshop on strategic problem solving and decision making (PSDM).

This chapter and the chapter that follows develop an array of PSDM competencies for use at the organization's strategic, operational, and tactical levels to confront a challenge, solve a problem, address an emerging issue, commit organizational resources, or select a course of action. You'll find these two chapters useful for big-picture issues (for example, should we enter this market?) as well as equally important but much smaller ones (for example, why are we losing our most capable staff to our competition?).

Objectives

As a result of participating in this workshop, participants will be able to

- identify common obstacles to effective PSDM

- apply the principles of effective PSDM to their own situations

- describe the seven-step model for strategic problem solving

- apply that model to a specific situation

- write a clear problem statement

- describe the seven-step model for strategic decision making

- discuss strategies and methods for involving diverse stakeholders in strategic PSDM.

Materials

For the instructor:

- Projector, screen, and computer for running the PowerPoint slides

- PowerPoint slides 9–1 through 9–35

- Learning Activity 11–19: Definitions and Distinctions

- Learning Activity 11–20: Exploring Our PSDM History

- Learning Activity 11–21: Principles to Guide Strategic PSDM

- Learning Activity 11–22: Approaches to PSDM

- Learning Activity 11–23: Applying the Strategic Problem-Solving Model

- Learning Activity 11–24: What Is Your Imagination Quotient?

- Learning Activity 11–25: Writing the Problem Statement

- Learning Activity 11–26: Applying the Strategic Decision-Making Model

- ◆ Learning Activity 11–27: Involving Others in Strategic PSDM

- ◆ Tool 12–1: Training Room Configuration and Layout

- ◆ Tool 12–4: Workshop Level 1 Evaluation

- ◆ Flipcharts, easels, and marking pens (one of each for every table)

For the participants:

- ◆ 3 x 5-inch index cards (one for each participant)

- ◆ Tool 12–2: Goal-Setting Worksheet

- ◆ Tool 12–3: Ah-Ha! Sheet

- ◆ Handouts and training instruments needed in the learning activities

Using the CD

Materials for this training session are provided either in this workbook or as electronic files on the accompanying CD. To access the electronic files, insert the CD and click on the appropriate Adobe .pdf document or PowerPoint .ppt/.pps file. Further directions and help using the files can be found in the appendix, "Using the Compact Disc," at the back of this workbook. Thumbnail versions of the PowerPoint slides for this workshop (*Strategic PSDM.ppt/.pps*) are included at the end of this chapter.

Preparation

Several months before the workshop:

1. Meet with representatives of the executive leadership team to discuss their expectations for the workshop. Integrate their ideas and perspectives as much as possible to ensure a good fit with existing approaches for PSDM in the organization and with the existing or emerging strategic plan.

2. Identify your target audience for this workshop, which serves as a stand-alone program for building basic PSDM knowledge and skills in frontline staff and managers.

3. Schedule the session and arrange for a training room. Ensure that the room can be configured to facilitate participant learning. See Tool 12–1 for a suggested room layout for the workshop.

4. Design the program, taking care to integrate the organization's current vision, core values, and strategic issues at appropriate times during the workshop. Decide if you will offer this course as a stand-alone or as the first of a two-day workshop (with Tools for Strategic Problem Solving and Decision Making, chapter 10, as the second day).

5. Prepare training materials. Customize them as needed to reflect any PSDM methods or processes currently in use in the organization. Familiarize yourself with the content and operation of all materials.

6. Send an invitation memo, letter, or e-mail to participants, reiterating the purpose of the workshop and its importance in helping participants deal with current issues, challenges, problems, and decisions.

7. Because you will want the workshop to reflect and address the real issues, challenges, and decisions that participants are facing in their daily work, you will want to customize the content of the workshop to the organization's real-world needs. Ask participants to identify two or three of the individual or organizational issues, challenges, or decisions they are facing. Gather this information *prior* to the workshop in one of two ways: (1) via memo or e-mail asking participants to send you a list of these pressing issues, challenges, problems, or decisions before the workshop; or (2) asking attendees to write this information on 3 x 5 index cards when they arrive at the training room. Decide the best way to gather this participant-specific information and then design the workshop to accommodate the method you use.

8. Order food and beverages as necessary.

Just prior to the workshop:

1. Arrive early at the training room.

2. Check room setup and make needed adjustments. Ensure that the room has enough space to allow for easy movement between tables and enough room for a flipchart easel to be placed next to each table.

3. Ensure that each table group will have access to a flipchart easel with paper and markers during the day. Place the easels on the periphery of the room initially and then move them in next to each table when needed.

4. Test equipment such as LCD and overhead projectors.

5. Prepare and post a flipchart page titled "Parking Lot" (if desired) and additional pages as called for in the learning activities. You may want to post another flipchart page highlighting key objective-related questions to be addressed during the workshop.

6. If you've chosen to gather participant-specific issues, challenges, problems, and pending decisions at the start of the workshop, place index cards for that purpose on group tables.

7. Display PowerPoint slide 9–1 as a welcome to participants and greet them individually as they enter the room.

Sample Agenda

8:30 a.m.   Welcome (10 minutes)

Kick off the session by displaying slide 9–2 as you talk through the three quotes there. Ask what is behind the wisdom in these quotes. Ask if participants find any of these particularly compelling or true for them.

With this as a context, welcome participants to the Workshop on Strategic Problem Solving and Decision Making, introduce yourself, and highlight the learning objectives of the workshop. Note that the focus of the session is building on the insights from these three people quoted on the slide.

Emphasize that this session is action oriented and that they will have an opportunity to apply models for PSDM to issues that the organization is currently facing.

Note the importance of this workshop dealing with the real issues and challenges that they face every day. If you asked participants to identify their issues in advance of the workshop, thank them for providing this information and note that you'll be using some of their issues in the day's workshop. If you chose to gather the information at the start of the workshop, point out the index cards on their tables. Display slide 9–3 and ask them to write on the cards one or two challenges or problems that the organization needs to address or decisions it needs to make in the near future. After a few minutes, ask everyone to pass their cards up to you.

8:40   Goal setting (20 minutes)

Explain that today's workshop strives to develop the key competencies involved with strategic PSDM.

Display slides 9–4, 9–5, and 9–6 and review the specific goals and road map for the day.

Distribute Tool 12–2 and ask participants to identify

◆   their individual objective for the workshop, and how likely it is that they will realize that objective in this session

◆   what's in it for them if they achieve their objective, and how likely it is that the reward will materialize

◆   how important this positive benefit or reward is to them.

After a couple of minutes, display slide 9–7 and ask participants to work in their small group to (1) meet and greet, (2) share their personal objectives (the first of the questions on the Goal-Setting Worksheet), and (3) identify two or three questions about strategic PSDM that the group would like to address during the workshop. Give the small groups approximately seven minutes for this activity.

Have the groups report their questions and record them on the prepared flipchart page. Highlight the importance of their taking responsibility for their own learning by exploring the answers to these questions as you work through the content of the session.

Point out that you have posted a Parking Lot as a place to record additional issues and questions that you may not be able to address today, and encourage them to post parking lot issues at any time.

Distribute Tool 12–3. Encourage them to be active participants in their own learning by using the Ah-Ha! Sheet to

record key learning moments and the insights that will be most useful to them beyond today's session.

Note the schedule for breaks and lunch, and the location of restrooms, telephones, and refreshments.

9:00   Learning Activity 11–19: Definitions and Distinctions (10 minutes)

This brief lecture introduces some simple definitions of a problem and a decision that will help anchor the day.

9:10   Learning Activity 11–20: Exploring Our PSDM History (25 minutes)

Developing more effective approaches to PSDM begins with a good understanding of why our methods sometimes work and sometimes don't. This learning activity engages participants in reflecting on their personal experience with PSDM in the organization, the reasons it works, the reasons it sometimes doesn't, and the consequences for the organization when it goes right or wrong.

9:35   Learning Activity 11–21: Principles to Guide Strategic PSDM (25 minutes)

This activity introduces principles that should guide strategic PSDM and asks participants to reflect on the extent to which their organization actually practices these principles.

10:00   Break (15 minutes)

10:15   Learning Activity 11–22: Approaches to PSDM (25 minutes)

This learning activity introduces two broad approaches to PSDM: the intuitive approach and the rational/analytical approach. It highlights the strengths and weaknesses of each and identifies when each is more appropriately used.

10:40   Learning Activity 11–23: Applying the Strategic Problem-Solving Model (70 minutes)

It's time to introduce a formal method for guiding the strategic problem-solving process. Remind participants that in this workshop they will explore both a model for strategic problem solving and a model for strategic decision making. Explain that you will first deal with problem solving—often a precursor step to decision making (the decision being which solution to implement).

This activity involves an overview of the strategic problem-solving model and an application of it to a common and presenting problem for the organization. Your advance preparation for this workshop involves identifying an example problem and preparing a PowerPoint slide and/or a flipchart page with the problem written out.

Warn the groups about 10 minutes before the break that, following the break, they will be expected to report their results.

11:20	Break (10 minutes)
11:30	Conclude the activity with the individual work groups reporting their recommended actions and discussing their reactions to using the problem-solving model.
Noon	Lunch (60 minutes)
1:00 p.m.	Learning Activity 11–24: What Is Your Imagination Quotient? (30 minutes)

To fight "post-lunch" sluggishness, start the afternoon off with this fun activity. It engages the group while it teaches some important points about thinking divergently, expansively, and outside the norm when they approach problem solving.

1:30 Learning Activity 11–25: Writing the Problem Statement (45 minutes)

Ninety percent of the challenge of solving a problem (strategically or otherwise) is getting the problem well defined. Building on the work accomplished in Learning Activity 11–23, this activity helps participants understand why groups may have arrived at different solutions for the same problem.

This exercise offers principles for writing good problem statements and has the groups working together to craft problem statements for some common organizational problems.

2:15   Break (15 minutes)

2:30   Learning Activity 11–26: Applying the Strategic Decision-Making Model (60 minutes)

Strategic decision making differs from strategic problem solving in that making a decision involves a choice among alternatives. Sometimes the decision involves a solution to a problem, sometimes it involves seizing the right strategic opportunity. And sometimes it involves something as simple (?) as deciding which copier to buy for the office!

This activity introduces a strategic decision-making model and engages participants in applying the model to a hypothetical decision.

3:30   Break (15 minutes)

3:45   Learning Activity 11–27: Involving Others in Strategic PSDM (25 minutes)

Strategic PSDM should almost always involve other people. Whether the level of others' participation demands that one gather information from others or that one allow them to solve the problem or make the decision on their own, reflecting on the nature and extent of participation is a key step in any strategic PSDM process.

The final learning activity for this workshop engages the groups and then the class as a whole in identifying situations and circumstances in which others should be included in a PSDM situation.

4:10   Review, integration, and question review (15 minutes)

Bring the workshop to a close by referring to the questions that the group asked at the beginning of the day. Review the questions as a large group and discuss any that remain unanswered. Whenever possible, ask the participants to offer their responses. As time permits, assign unanswered questions to individual groups and give them four minutes to develop a response.

4:25　　　Evaluation (5 minutes)

Display slide 9–35. Thank everyone for attending the workshop and for being actively involved all day.

Distribute Tool 12–4 and encourage participants to leave the completed forms at their seats or a designated location.

4:30　　　Close

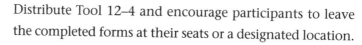

What to Do Next

◆　Prepare for the full-day session on strategic PSDM.

◆　Customize the learning activities and materials you will use to ensure that the workshop reflects the organization's actual and anticipated strategic-planning practices.

◆　Compile the learning activities, handouts, training instruments, tools, and PowerPoint slides you will use in the training and thoroughly familiarize yourself with their content.

◆　Decide whether to offer the additional one-day workshop on the tools for strategic PSDM (chapter 10).

◆ ◆ ◆

The next chapter presents a one-day workshop on the tools for strategic PSDM. You will find that this follow-on workshop offers practical tools that people can use within the strategic PSDM models that they have learned in this chapter.

Slide 9–1

Strategic Problem Solving and Decision Making

Approaches for Bringing Strategic Focus to Organizational Problem Solving and Decision Making

Slide 9-1

Slide 9–2

"No problem is so large or complex that it can't be run away from."
— Charlie Brown

"There is always an easy solution to every human problem — neat, plausible, and wrong."
— H. L. Mencken

"The most common source of mistakes in management decisions is the emphasis on finding the right answers rather than the right question."
— Peter Drucker

Slide 9–3

The Challenges We Face

Working by yourself . . .

– Identify one or two unsolved challenges or problems facing the organization today, or one or two decisions that need to be made in the near future.

– When you have completed your card, gather them at your tables and pass them to the trainer.

Note: We'll try to use some of the challenges, problems, or decisions you identify in today's workshop.

Slide 9-3

Slide 9–4

Learning Objectives

■ Identify common obstacles to effective problem solving and decision making

■ Apply the principles of effective problem solving and decision making to real-life situations

■ Describe the seven-step model for strategic problem solving

■ Apply the strategic problem-solving model to a specific situation

■ Write a clear problem statement

■ Describe the seven-step model for strategic decision making

■ Discuss strategies and methods for involving diverse stakeholders in strategic problem solving and decision making

Slide 9-4

Slide 9–5

Morning Learning Agenda

• Exploring our problem solving and decision making history

• Identifying principles of problem solving and decision making

• Describing two broad approaches to problem solving and decision making

• Applying the problem-solving model

Slide 9-5

Slide 9–6

Afternoon Learning Agenda

• Writing a problem statement

• Applying the strategic decision-making model

• Involving others in problem solving and decision making

Slide 9-6

Slide 9–7

Meet and Greet!

● Introduce yourself to your table partners.

● Share your personal objective(s) for the day.

● As a group . . . identify some common goals/issues of interest.

● Develop two or three questions about strategic problem solving and decision making that your group would like to have answered before the end of the day.

Slide 9-7

Slide 9–8

What is a _problem_?

What is a _decision_?

Slide 9-8

Slide 9–9

A Problem Is . . .

an absence or void that remains until an appropriate response is found.

A problem exists in situations where an individual or group fails to find an effective way to meet or fulfill a need of a person, group, community, or society.

Slide 9-9

Slide 9–10

A Decision Is . . .

a <u>choice</u> made from among alternative solutions or options when faced with solving a problem, fulfilling an unmet need, or finding the best way to achieve a goal or an aspiration.

Slide 9-10

Slide 9–11

Our PSDM History

On your own . . .

– Identify an example in the organization in which problem solving or decision making went very well. _Why_ did it go well? What were the consequences of its going well?

– Identify an example in the organization in which problem solving or decision making did<u>NOT</u> go well. _Why_ didn't it go well? And what were the consequences of this less desirable result?

Slide 9-11

Slide 9–12

Our PSDM History

As a small group . . .

– Share your PSDM histories.

– Identify trends or themes in _successful_ PSDM. What were some causes of good PSDM outcomes? What were the consequences?

– Identify trends or themes for _unsuccessful_ PSDM. What were the causes? What were the consequences?

Slide 9-12

Slide 9-13

Seven Breakthrough-Thinking Principles for PSDM

1. Approach each problem for its uniqueness.
2. Define your purpose.
3. Explore the "solution after next."
4. Use systems thinking.
5. Limit your data gathering.
6. Involve diverse perspectives.
7. Revisit the solution, the problem, and the solution after next.

Slide 9-14

The Seven Principles of Breakthrough Thinking

On your own . . .

- Which principle does this organization do a pretty good job of practicing in its approach to decision making and problem solving?

- Which principle does this organization tend <u>not</u> to practice?

Slide 9-15

The Seven Principles of Breakthrough Thinking

In your small group, discuss . . .

- Which principle the organization tends to follow and practice.

- Which principle the organization tends <u>NOT</u> to follow or practice.

- For the principle identified in the second question, identify actions that individuals could take to increase the use/application of this principle throughout the organization.

Slide 9-16

Approaches to PSDM

- Intuitive Approach — Solving a problem through intuition, insight, "gut" feelings, and divergent thinking

- Rational/Analytical Approach — Solving a problem through a formally structured, systematic, methodical, and scientific process.

Slide 9-17

When to Use Each Approach

In your small group, for your assigned approach, . . .

– Identify the strengths and weaknesses of this approach.

– Identify when to use and NOT use each approach.

Slide 9-18

A Problem-Solving Model

1. Select and define the problem.
   - Narrow the problem
   - Identify whom to involve
2. Define desired outcomes, higher purpose and measurement.
   - Identify measures of success
3. Identify potential causes.
4. Identify potential roadblocks.
5. Identify actions to address causes.
6. Develop an action plan.
7. Implement, monitor, evaluate, and revise.

Slide 9-19

What influenced your problem solving?

Slide 9-20

Factors That Influence the Problem-Solving Process

- Who was involved (and the knowledge level of the problem)
- What information you had available to you
- Time available
- Experience with or knowledge of the problem
- Group dynamics
- Group size
- Problem solving history as a group
- ???

Slide 9-21

Your Imagination Quotient

- What is your IQ?
- Work as a team to solve these "out-of-the-box" puzzlers.
- Work quickly to be the first group to complete the IQ quiz.

Slide 9-22

Inside or Outside?

Slide 9-23

Young or Seasoned?

Slide 9-24

In the Shadows . . . .

Slide 9–25

Connecting the Dots . . .

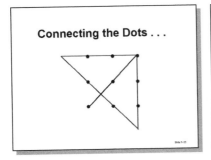

Slide 9–26

It's so much easier to suggest solutions when you don't know too much about the problem.

— Malcolm Forbes
U.S. business leader

Slide 9–27

Writing the Problem Statement

❏ State the problem objectively. Focus on the facts: what is *known* vs. what is *assumed.*
❏ Address the questions: *What isn't working? What isn't right? Why is this an issue we need to pay attention to?*
❏ Avoid *implied* causes and *implied* solutions
❏ Narrow the scope of the problem
❏ Identify the relationship of the problem to *other* problems
❏ Develop a *shared* vision of the problem
❏ Develop a *shared* vision of the outcome

Slide 9–28

Sample Problem Statements

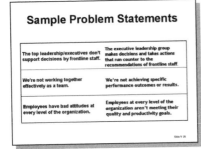

Slide 9–29

Sample Problem Statements

Operator errors create unacceptable levels of scrap.	How can we improve product quality and employee productivity in our manufacturing process?
Our new product rollout was a total failure because of a lack of understanding of the customers' needs.	Our new product rollout failed to meet our sales targets for three of the last four quarters.
This new generation of workers has an unrealistic idea of what it takes to move up the organizational ladder.	New employees (ages 19-25) tend to express higher levels of frustration with the organization's career paths.

Slide 9–30

The Decision-Making Process

1. Define the decision you want to make.
   Narrow the decision
   Identify whom to involve
2. Define your desired outcomes, strategic objectives, and higher purpose.
   Identify measures of success
   Sort out your musts and wants, rank-ordering wants from most to least and assigning values (1–10) to each
3. Identify decision alternatives and options.
4. Select the best alternative.
5. Identify potential roadblocks/setbacks.
6. Develop an action/implementation plan.
7. Implement the plan, monitor progress, and revise the plan.

Slide 9–31

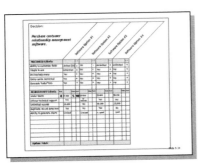

Slide 9–32

Involving Others

- When is it desirable to involve others?
- When might it *not* be as desirable or appropriate to involve others?

Slide 9–33

Involving Others

Autocratic   I decide

Democratic   We decide

You decide   Empowered

Slide 9–34

Involving Others

Participation is important because

1. It increases the likelihood of defining the problem/decision correctly and understanding the context of the problem/decision—including the underlying causes—and identifying critical *must/want* needs.
2. It can powerfully and positively influence the level of commitment to the decision or solution in those asked to implement the decision or solution.

Slide 9–35

Thank You!

- Integrate the principles of problem solving and decision making into your daily practice.
- Apply the problem-solving model to your everyday situations.
- Practice the decision-making model and use the decision matrix to help define your decision requirements.
- Reflect on the opportunities and strategies for involving others in PSDM.

One-Day Workshop: Tools for Strategic Problem Solving and Decision Making

- List of objectives for the one-day workshop on tools for strategic problem solving and decision making

- Lists of materials for instructor and participants

- Detailed instructions on workshop preparation

- Workshop agenda and facilitator's guide

This chapter presents a workshop that highlights some of the most practical and accessible tools to use within strategic problem solving and decision making (PSDM). Because the tools are flexible and adaptable, they can be used with any of the other workshop designs in this book—or as stand-alone tools applied to a wide array of organizational challenges.

This is a lively and engaging workshop in which participants tackle real issues facing their organization. As with some of the earlier workshop designs, the results from using the tools in this chapter can be used as part of either formulating or updating a strategic plan, or to generate some strategies for dealing with tough operational or tactical challenges.

Objectives

As a result of participating in this workshop, participants will be able to

- identify more than a dozen tools and methods for strategic PSDM and know when use of each is appropriate

- practice and apply at least six of the tools to the issues, challenges, or problems currently facing the organization

♦ discuss the strengths and weaknesses of each of the tools

♦ identify future opportunities for applying the tools to their own situations, challenges, and opportunities.

Materials

For the instructor:

♦ Projector, screen, and computer for running the PowerPoint slides

♦ PowerPoint slides 10–1 through 10–18

♦ Learning Activity 11–28: Introducing the Strategic PSDM Tool Kit and Prioritizing the Tools

♦ Learning Activity 11–29: Applying the Strategic PSDM Tools

♦ Learning Activity 11–30: Personal Action Planning

♦ Tool 12–1: Training Room Configuration and Layout

♦ Tool 12–4: Workshop Level 1 Evaluation

♦ Flipcharts, easels, and marking pens (one of each for every group and two or three flipcharts for your own use during the workshop)

♦ Whiteboard or paper, 4 x 12 feet, and appropriate markers. The larger the writing space, the better; but this activity can be done on smaller work surfaces. Use newsprint or butcher paper, or tape together several sheets of flipchart paper.

For the participants:

♦ 3 x 3-inch sticky-notes and fine-point, felt-tip marking pens (one for each participant)

♦ 3 x 5-inch index cards (one for each group)

♦ Half-inch sticky-dots (one red and four blue for each participant)

♦ Handout 11–23: A Model for Problem Solving

♦ Handout 11–25: A Model for Strategic Decision Making

♦ Handout 11–28: Strategic PSDM Tool Kit

♦ Handouts and training instruments needed in the learning activities

Using the CD

Materials for this training session are provided either in this workbook or as electronic files on the accompanying CD. To access the electronic files, insert the CD and click on the appropriate Adobe .pdf document or PowerPoint .ppt/.pps file. Further directions and help using the files can be found in the appendix, "Using the Compact Disc," at the back of this workbook. Thumbnail versions of the PowerPoint slides for this workshop (*Tools.ppt/.pps*) are included at the end of this chapter.

Preparation

Several months before the workshop:

1. Schedule the session and arrange for a training room. Ensure that the room is large enough to accommodate the audience size with five or six people at each small-group table. Also ensure that the room has a large whiteboard (at least 4 x 12 feet) or an expanse of uninterrupted wall space large enough for posting a paper wallchart. See Tool 12–1 for a suggested room layout for the workshop.

2. Develop a list of likely issues, challenges, problems, and decisions that the organization is currently facing. These issues can emerge from your needs assessment process (chapter 3), the request you sent to participants attending the Strategic Problem Solving and Decision Making Workshop (chapter 9), the executive leadership or strategic-planning team, or they may be based on your own experience with the organization.

   If the executive leadership or strategic-planning team has given you a list of issues that it wants the workshop to explore, you will need to design the workshop to ensure that these are addressed. Even if the executive leadership or strategic-planning team has given you its issues for the workshop, however, you are still strongly encouraged to design the workshop so that there is an opportunity for the participants to identify additional issues (strategic or operational) that they are facing. Refine your list of issues and summarize them in a handout or flipchart page that you create for the session, or on a PowerPoint slide.

   Whatever the source, use the issues to help you prepare examples and relevant exercises for the workshop. Although the initial learning activity in the course has participants identify issues, challenges, and decisions, preparing your own list in advance will help you select issues that are likely to be chosen. It will also enable you to decide in advance which tools you will use for tackling which issues, challenges, and decisions.

3. Design the program around the organization's objectives. This workshop can be designed as a stand-alone program to simply enable participants to practice each PSDM tool, or it can be designed to support the use of the tools within a more formal strategic-planning process.

4. For each tool in the Strategic PSDM Tool Kit (Handout 11–28), identify one or more possible organizational issues that could be explored using the tool. This is particularly important for the Decision Matrix, which requires considerable advance preparation—especially in identifying the decision choices/options and the decision requirements. The pre-work you do for the Decision Matrix and all of the other tools will ensure that you have a ready example for the use of each tool.

5. Prepare training materials and familiarize yourself with their content and use. Gather stationery supplies specified in the learning activities.

6. Send an invitation memo, letter, or e-mail to participants, reiterating the purpose of the workshop and its importance in helping them deal with the real issues and challenges (both operational and strategic) facing them every day.

7. Order food and beverages as necessary.

Just prior to the workshop:

1. Arrive early at the training room.

2. Check room setup and make needed adjustments.

3. Set out flipcharts and easels, and test equipment such as LCD and overhead projectors. Until needed, the easels can be placed around the room's periphery. When they are moved into position beside each table, be sure to position them so they don't impede anyone's line of sight and so that there is ample space to move among the tables.

4. Prepare and post appropriate flipchart pages and the whiteboard or wallchart as detailed in the learning activities.

5. Place sticky-dots, sticky-notes, and marking pens on tables.

6. Display PowerPoint slide 10–1 as a welcome to participants and greet them individually as they enter the room.

Sample Agenda

8:30 a.m. Welcome (5 minutes)

Welcome participants to the Tools for Strategic Problem Solving and Decision Making Workshop. Introduce yourself and highlight the day's learning objectives as you display slide 10–2.

Note that this session will develop their use and application of a wide variety of practical tools both within a strategic framework and in their daily actions and interactions.

If this workshop follows the one-day workshop on Strategic Problem Solving and Decision Making (chapter 9), make the connection between the larger method for PSDM and the practical tools for successfully navigating these two methodologies.

8:35 Identifying the challenges we face (40 minutes)

This introduction is key to the workshop in that it will give you and the participants specific issues, challenges, problems, and decisions to work with during the day. Although you already may have a list of issues that the group might address (see preparation step 3), asking participants to identify some issues they are facing will help anchor the workshop in their own experience.

If the executive leadership or strategic-planning team has given you specific issues that it wants the group to address, share this list of issues at this point in the workshop (in the form of an additional handout, a flipchart page, or a PowerPoint slide).

Display slide 10–3 and ask participants to work in small groups to identify the top two or three items facing the organization today. Ask them either to prioritize the list of issues, challenges, problems, and decisions you have already given them or to identify additional matters. Have groups record their top two or three issues on the index card on each table.

After five minutes, reconvene the large group and ask a member of each small group to report its top-priority issues. Facilitate a discussion exploring the sentiments of each group so that you get a better understanding of the most critical issues.

Ask the groups to pass their completed index cards to you. The resulting list of real issues will be used in practicing the strategic PSDM tools during the session. With real issues, participants' interest level is likely to remain high. **Note:** Workshops driven by participant-identified issues will produce results that can be used by attendees and by the entire organization in situations beyond the training room.

9:15   Exploring our past experience with tools for PSDM (25 minutes)

Ask participants to work in groups for five minutes to identify specific tools and techniques they have used or have seen used for PSDM in the organization. Display slide 10–4 with specific instructions for the groups.

While the groups work, prepare a flipchart page titled *PSDM Tools and Techniques* for use when the groups report their findings.

Reconvene the whole class and ask participants to report what PSDM tools they have used; write them on the flipchart page. After all of the tools, techniques, or methods have been listed, ask how useful each has been at facilitating effective PSDM. Ask if any of the tools identified were poorly used or if they had failed to assist in good PSDM.

Summarize this discussion by noting that within the PSDM process, one of the primary reasons why the results aren't always what we want them to be is the failure to practice methods and tools that help clarify our thinking, remove our personal bias as much as possible, and limit the influence of one or two individuals on the outcome. Indicate that the class will be working with some of the tools they've already used and with some new tools that will strengthen their PSDM processes. Point out that using the right tools in the right way for the right purpose can significantly and positively influence the quality of both the PSDM processes and their outcomes.

9:40   PSDM models (25 minutes)

Build on the past activity and explain that the tools attendees will be using today are best understood in the context of the two PSDM processes and through actual practice. Indicate that you want to offer a brief overview of the two PSDM processes.

Distribute Handouts 11–23 and 11–25. If this workshop follows the one-day Strategic Problem Solving and Decision Making Workshop (chapter 9), point out that this handout was shared with them earlier and emphasize the importance of bringing practical tools to both processes. If this is a stand-alone workshop, explain that they won't actively be exploring the details of these two models in today's session, but that the tools they practice today will help them solve problems effectively and make good decisions by using a more thoughtful and deliberate approach.

Begin the overview of the two processes by displaying slide 10–5. Highlight the key steps of the problem-solving process. Note that, for each step, problem solvers need to bring the best insights and perspectives from the diverse stakeholders who are involved in or affected by the problem. Highlight the importance of exploring the *causes* and explain that the solutions to a problem largely focus on addressing these causes. Ask if anyone has any questions about the problem-solving model before moving to the decision-making process.

Display slide 10–6. Highlight the key steps of the decision-making process. Note the differences between the problem-solving method and this step-by-step process for making a decision (making a choice from among alternatives or choosing a course of action). Point out the importance of identifying and *quantifying* one's decision requirements and desires. Ask if anyone has any questions about the decision-making model.

Summarize this segment of the workshop by noting that effective strategic PSDM requires a thoughtful and disciplined approach that encourages divergent thinking. Point out that the tools learned today can help create an environment that promotes divergent thinking and integrates all of this diversity into a shared understanding of the problem, decision, causes, and potential solutions.

10:05   Break (15 minutes)

10:20   Learning Activity 11–28: Introducing the Strategic PSDM Tool Kit and Prioritizing the Tools (30 minutes)

Distribute Handout 11–28: Strategic PSDM Tool Kit. This activity reinforces the step-by-step PSDM models discussed in the previous segment and identifies a variety of tools that participants can use within the two processes. It also engages participants in prioritizing the PSDM tools using sticky-dots.

10:50   Learning Activity 11–29: Applying the Tools (215 minutes total; 70 minutes this segment)

This learning activity is the primary focus for the rest of this workshop. Participants practice applying the tools that they selected (in the previous learning activity) to specific organizational issues.

Note: Because the activity will be interrupted by lunch and an afternoon break, the amount of time listed for each segment is flexible. Try to choose natural breaks in the rhythm of the activity as times for lunch and the mid-afternoon break.

Noon   Lunch (60 minutes)

1:00 p.m.   Learning Activity 11–29, continued (75 minutes this segment)

Continue along the list of tools, as selected by participants in Learning Activity 11–28.

2:15   Break (15 minutes)

2:30   Learning Activity 11–29, continued (55 minutes this segment)

Guide the groups through the last of the tools for which you have time during the workshop.

3:25   Break (15 minutes)

3:40   Learning Activity 11–29, concluded (15 minutes)

Reconvene the large group and highlight the array of tools and issues that they have tackled and applied today. If arrangements have been made in advance to do so, note that the results from the tool applications will be transcribed and forwarded to them and to other appropriate organizational stakeholders.

Stress the practical application of these tools as evident in the range of organizational challenges that they handled in the session. Encourage them to continue using the tools for their strategic and operational planning and for the simple and complex issues they face.

3:55   Learning Activity 11–30: Personal Action Planning (30 minutes)

Make the transition to this final activity by stressing the importance of their developing a personal plan for applying the tools learned to their daily work.

4:25   Evaluation (5 minutes)

End the workshop by displaying slide 10–18. Thank participants for attending and for their active involvement throughout the session. Distribute Tool 12–4 and encourage participants to leave the completed forms at their tables or another designated location.

4:30   Close

What to Do Next

- ◆ Prepare for the one-day session covering the PSDM Tool Kit.

- ◆ Customize the learning activities and materials you will use to ensure that the workshop reflects the organization's actual and anticipated strategic-planning practices.

- ◆ Compile the learning activities, handouts, training instruments, tools, and PowerPoint slides you will use in the training and thoroughly familiarize yourself with their content.

- ◆ Develop a list of potential or likely organizational issues, challenges, and decisions that need to be made. You will use this list to prepare examples for use in Learning Activity 11–29. The list can also serve as your fall-back set of issues in case the group doesn't identify enough specific issues, challenges, problems, or decisions at the beginning of the workshop.

Slide 10–1

Tools for Strategic Problem Solving and Decision Making

Practical Methods and Tools

Slide 10–2

Learning Objectives

- Identify more than a dozen tools/methods for strategic problem solving and decision making.
- Practice and apply at least six of the tools to the issues, challenges, or problems currently facing your organization.
- Discuss the strengths and weaknesses of each of the tools.
- Identify future opportunities for applying the tools to current and future situations, challenges, and opportunities.

Slide 10–3

The Challenges We Face . . .

As a small group . . .

- Develop a list of the key issues, challenges, problems, or decisions that our organization faces today.
- From this list, identify the top two or three issues.
- Write your top issue on the index card

Slide 10–4

Tools for PSDM

Reflect on your experience with PSDM in your professional life.

- What specific tools, techniques, or methods have you used in your PSDM?
- How effective have these tools and methods been for you? Did they improve the quality of your PSDM process? Did they lead you to good outcomes?

Slide 10–5

A Problem-Solving Model . . .

1. Select and define the problem.
   — Narrow the problem
   — Identify whom to involve
2. Define desired outcomes, higher purpose and measurement.
   — Identify measures of success
3. Identify potential causes.
4. Identify potential roadblocks.
5. Identify actions to address causes.
6. Develop an action plan.
7. Implement, monitor, evaluate, and revise.

Slide 10–6

The Decision-Making Process

1. Define the decision you want to make.
   — Narrow the decision
   — Identify whom to involve
2. Define your desired outcomes, strategic objectives, and higher purpose.
   — Identify measures of success
   — Sort out your musts and wants, rank-ordering wants from most to least and assign values (1–10) to each
3. Identify decision alternatives and options.
4. Select the best alternative.
5. Identify potential roadblocks/setbacks.
6. Develop an action/implementation plan.
7. Implement the plan, monitor progress, and revise the plan.

Slide 10–7

PSDM Tools

The PSDM Toolkit

- contains some of the most useful and accessible tools for PSDM
- describes purpose of each tool, when appropriate, and how to use each
- identifies when each tool is used within the PSDM processes

---

Slide 10–8

Voting for the PSDM Tools

- Read "What is [tool name]?" for each of the ten PSDM tools.
- On your own, identify the five tools (of the eight listed) that you would most like to practice today.
- Vote for your top five tools — the RED dot reflects your *highest*-priority tool, the four BLUE dots are your *second*-priority tools.
- Place your dots on the prepared flipchart page.

Slide 10–9

Brainstorming Principles

- Go for *quantity*.
- Share ideas in headline style.
- Don't judge, argue over, criticize, praise, or evaluate the ideas offered.
- Build on or combine each other's ideas.
- Remember that wild, off-the-wall, and humorous ideas stimulate creative thinking.
- Encourage everyone to participate—but silence is okay, too.

Slide 10–10

Cause→Effect Diagram

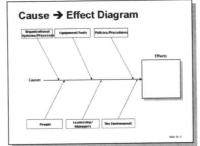

Slide 10–11

Cause → Effect Diagram

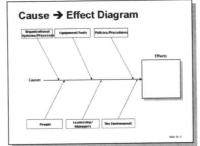

Slide 10–12

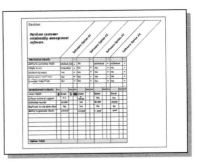

Slide 10–13

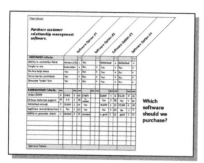

Slide 10–14

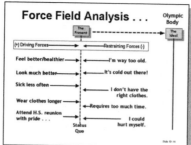

Slide 10–15

Is/Is Not Matrix

	The Problem IS	The Problem IS Not
What?	Late for deadlines	Quality of work
Where?	On projects that involve other people	On projects where she works by herself
When?	The last two weeks of every month	The first two weeks of every month
How Big?	60% of her projects	40% of her projects

Slide 10–16

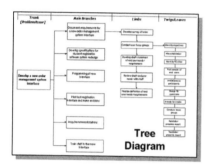

Tree Diagram

Slide 10–17

Developing Your Plan

- Identify one or two key issues, challenges, or decisions that you face.
- Identify one or more PSDM tools you could use for each issue.
- Identify how the tool will be useful to you.

Slide 10–18

Continuing Your Learning

- Practice and apply the tools for problem solving and decision making to your everyday situations.
- Take risks. Try out a new tool, even when you're not sure that it will work.
- Teach others how to use the tools. Don't try to do this alone!
- When you have mastered these tools, explore the use of other PSDM tools from other books and sources.

◆

Learning Activities

- ◆ Tips for trainers and training program designers

- ◆ Detailed step-by-step instructions for presenting the learning activities called for in the sample workshops in chapters 6 through 10

This chapter presents all of the learning activities identified in the sample workshop agendas in chapters 6 through 10. Each learning activity includes the following information:

- ◆ **Objectives:** The objectives are the primary affective, behavioral, or cognitive outcomes that the activity is attempting to achieve for participants.

- ◆ **Materials:** Listed here is everything the trainer will need to successfully conduct that activity. On the accompanying CD you will find every handout, tool, or training instrument called for in the activities. They can be printed from the appropriate .pdf files there. For most activities, however, we recommend that handouts be customized to fit the needs of the organization.

- ◆ **Time:** We offer a suggested number of minutes to complete the learning activity. This time includes introducing the activity, the exercise itself, and debriefing and transitioning to the next learning activity.

- ◆ **Preparation:** These are brief instructions for the trainer in advance of the activity—such things as copying materials, defining a situation or case, preparing flipchart pages, or arranging the training room to accommodate specific exercises.

◆ **Instructions:** We provide step-by-step directions for guiding participants through the activity. Key points you should make, likely reactions or answers from participants, and suggested responses to participant questions are included here. Process variations may also be included.

◆ **Debriefing:** This section guides you in helping participants integrate the activity into their learning. By offering key summary points, posing integrating or synthesizing questions to participants, or guiding their action planning, you can significantly strengthen learning and move learners to the next activity.

Tips for Trainers and Program Designers

Designing and delivering a high-quality training program involves blending these suggested workshop agendas, handouts, tools, training instruments, and PowerPoint slides with your own knowledge, experience, and insights. You also need a solid grounding in the broader topic of strategic planning. We strongly encourage you to read and then reread chapter 2 to gain a comfort level with the various approaches to strategic planning and some of its challenges. Reading one or more of the recommended texts—especially Henry Mintzberg's *The Rise and Fall of Strategic Planning* (1994) and *Strategy Safari* (1998)—will help you develop greater depth in the research and thinking behind the various models and approaches to strategic planning.

You will also need to become deeply familiar with your organization's strategic-planning methodology and practice. There are countless variations on the planning models, and you must know the unique practice that your organization uses. If, however, the organization is looking to you for direction on best practices and what method or approach it should use, your research into the topic can be helpful to the executive leadership and strategic-planning teams.

The sample workshop agendas, handouts, tools, and training instruments should be the jumping-off spot for your own design. They can never substitute for your unique experience or style. Become familiar enough with each workshop design that you can tell your own stories, offer your own examples, and incorporate recent events and circumstances in the organization. Participants need to see that the workshop design and content reflect what is real for them. Increase the likelihood of this happening by investing design time that puts the organization's stamp on the workshop.

You will also find it invaluable to take the up-front time to assess the organization's attitudes and perceptions of strategic planning and thinking and to identify some of the issues that it will face ahead as it develops its strategic plan. Exploring the answers to the needs assessment questions included in chapter 3 will be key in designing your training program. You will find, however, that the answers can be fed into the organization's strategic-planning process itself to refine and strengthen it. This is where your strategic organizational development role beyond training is most effective.

You may find, for example, that training in strategic planning and PSDM should be postponed until deeper, more systemic or structural issues are dealt with. Perhaps your inquiry will uncover a perception among key stakeholders that any strategic PSDM process will be undercut by the CEO or chief operating officer with a personal agenda. Rather than introducing a strategic-planning or problem-solving methodology through skill-building workshops, your efforts might shift to developing greater openness and critical thinking among members of the executive leadership team. This, of course, is only one example of how you might need to adjust your skill building to what you learn from your needs assessment. The important thing is first to slow down and define the real need—and then design the best array of organizational development and training activities to meet that need.

Finally, as you begin putting together your own workshop design for whatever training you finally decide to offer, stay flexible. The estimated timeframes offered for each learning activity can and should be changed according to what you learn in your needs assessment, the goals for the session, your own personal style, the examples and cases you introduce, the stories you have to share, the personality of the organization or training group, and where the executive leadership or strategic-planning team wants you to focus.

You will find that, as your confidence and competence in delivering the workshops in this book increase and as you receive feedback from participants, your training design will continue to improve. Don't expect to get it 100 percent right the first time out. Reflect on what worked and what didn't (based on feedback and your own intuition), and then make the appropriate adjustments. As with good PSDM, the process of training program design involves combining discipline in the process with your instincts and experience.

We are confident that the training programs that emerge from this living process will hit their marks. People will learn; your organization will learn; and your own learning as an HRD professional will continue.

Learning Activity 11–1: Ensuring Organizational Success

OBJECTIVES

The objectives of this learning activity are to

- ◆ identify participant perceptions of the key factors that contribute to long-term organizational success

- ◆ challenge the perception that planning protects the organization from failure or ensures its long-term success

- ◆ highlight the results from research into the characteristics that tend to increase organizational longevity.

MATERIALS

- ◆ PowerPoint slides 6–2 through 6–6

- ◆ Handout 11–1: Fallacies of Strategic Planning

- ◆ Handout 11–2: Characteristics of Enduring Organizations

- ◆ Training Instrument 11–1: Ensuring Organizational Success

- ◆ Flipchart and marking pens

TIME

- ◆ 25 minutes

PREPARATION

- ◆ Prepare a single flipchart page titled *What Ensures the Long-Term Success of an Organization?*

INSTRUCTIONS

1. Display slide 6–2 and distribute Training Instrument 11–1. Ask the full class to offer ideas on what ensures the longevity of any organization. As people give their ideas (for example, *leadership, good people, a product/service valued by customers, profits, ability to change with the times, teamwork, communication,* or *a strategic plan*), write them on

the flipchart page you prepared earlier. Give them about a minute for this.

2. Now dramatically display slide 6–3 as you say something like, "Here's the secret to long-term organizational success!" Tell them to quickly copy this flowchart down because it's not included in the handouts for today's session. (*Be sure to indicate that you are only joking*—especially if people actually start sketching the diagram. Most of the time, participants will laugh when they first see the diagram and will recognize that it isn't really the answer to the question.)

3. Suggest that this diagram, adapted from the "Planning School" of strategy formation, represented a way of thinking about strategy formation some 40 years ago and that the principles and practices from this school are still followed by many organizations. There is, however, very little evidence that following all the paths on the flowchart actually leads to better organizational results. Suggest that a number of fundamental flaws in the thinking behind this model undercut its effectiveness.

4. Ask participants to tell you what they think might be problematic with the approach represented by the diagram. (**Note:** Most of the diagram won't be readable but that's OK. The point isn't to read it but to recognize the fallacy that planning and implementation is a substitute for good insight, intuition, foresight, and strategy formulation.) They may offer such responses as these: *too complicated, too confusing, too rigid, doesn't reflect how the real world works, takes too long to do, requires experts, don't know where to begin.*

5. Reinforce participants' ideas. Point out that your initial question was a trick question: There is no way to ensure organizational longevity. There are no guarantees of organizational success. There can be no assurances that any organization will exist for the long term. Explain that the research into organizational longevity suggests that most of us will outlive the organizations we work for (see chapter 2 for pertinent information).

6. Distribute Handout 11–1 and display and walk them through slides   6–4 and 6–5. As you begin these slides, say that in the real world of organizations, a different set of principles applies than those of the exclusively rational/analytical planning school.

7. Summarize this handout and these slides by suggesting that the point of strategic planning is to help create a level of awareness, understanding, and learning throughout an organization so that two positive results occur: (1) individuals in the organization become more adept at strategic thinking, and (2) by developing strategic thinkers at every level, the organization is more able to understand, anticipate, and prepare for environmental changes and take the appropriate strategic actions that move it closer toward its vision—to what it seeks to accomplish or create in the world.

8. Move toward a discussion of Handout 11–2 by suggesting that the pursuit of organizational longevity is best accomplished by exploring the factors that seem to contribute most to enabling some organizations to survive (even thrive) while others whither and disappear. Display slide 6–6 as you distribute Handout 11–2 and point out what research has found to be characteristics of enduring organizations.

DEBRIEFING

◆ Suggest that this opening activity has challenged some fundamental assumptions about strategic planning and has introduced the importance of strategic thinking in the real world.

◆ Note that the balance of today (and, if appropriate, the following workshop—Advanced Issues in Strategic Planning and Thinking) explores practical ideas and methods for developing real-world plans that engage people at every organizational level in strategic thinking and learning that, in turn, lead to more effective strategic action.

◆ Emphasize that, although traditional approaches to strategic planning may be dead, their demise opens up an entire world of possibilities for helping our organizations navigate the choppy waters of an uncertain future.

◆ Stress that today's workshop (and those that may follow) will strengthen and broaden the key strategic-thinking competencies at all levels of the organization to increase its chances of surviving for the long term.

Learning Activity 11–2:
Perceptions of Strategic Planning

OBJECTIVES

The objectives of this learning activity are to

- quickly identify existing perceptions of and attitudes toward strategic planning

- highlight both the benefits and potential downsides of developing a strategic plan

- emphasize the importance of avoiding the downsides and maximizing the benefits of strategic planning.

MATERIALS

- PowerPoint slide 6–9

- Training Instrument 11–2: Perceptions of Strategic Planning

- Flipchart and marking pens

TIME

- 20 minutes

PREPARATION

- Prepare a flipchart page with the two columns shown in Training Instrument 11–2.

INSTRUCTIONS

1. Distribute Training Instrument 11–2 and display slide 6–9. Ask participants to turn to the instrument and reflect on their experience with and exposure to strategic planning—in their current position with the organization or with previous organizations. Invite them to follow the instructions on the page and list both their positive perceptions of strategic planning and their negative impressions. Give them two minutes to do this.

2. Call the group's attention to the flipchart you prepared. Invite them first to share some positive perceptions of strategic planning. Have

them complete the statement, *Strategic planning is great because....* Likely responses include *it's an opportunity for improvement, it offers something new, it produces learning, it addresses problem areas, it's a way of staying close to the customer, it helps you make better decisions, it reminds us of what's important.*

3. When you have developed the positives list, shift the group's attention to the negatives list. Ask participants to share their negative perceptions of strategic planning—the potential traps or downfalls that can come with the development of a plan. Have them complete the statement, *Strategic planning can be a problem when it....* Participants may offer such ideas as *takes too long, is too rigid and inflexible, just collects dust on the shelf, doesn't reflect the real world, moves us in the wrong direction, limits our choices, is developed only by upper management, doesn't make room for unplanned events, only addresses profits [or some other single dimension] rather than multiple priorities, is too focused on control, is ignored.*

4. When you have completed both the positive and negative columns on the flipchart, ask for comments, observations, and reactions. Ask if they think the lists might be different in another organization.

DEBRIEFING

◆ Complete the perceptions of strategic planning activity by suggesting to participants that how this organization approaches the development of its strategic plan, who it involves, and how the plan is implemented make all the difference in how the plan will be perceived and, more important, whether it avoids the fate of plans that end up in the right-hand column.

◆ Note that the strategic plan is only as good as the process an organization uses to develop and maintain the plan's vitality.

◆ Remind participants that they can increase the likelihood of developing a plan that avoids the pitfalls listed in the right-hand column by being aware of the pitfalls and using a thoughtful process.

◆ Explain that there are no guarantees that a strategic plan will end up in either column. It takes the right people, the right mindset, a clear approach, a disciplined process, and hard work to develop an effective plan.

◆ Indicate that the next learning activity defines strategic planning and the contents of a strategic plan. Remind them to keep these positive and negative perceptions in mind as they explore the components of a plan and better understand how to develop it.

Learning Activity 11–3: Definition and Key Components of Strategic Planning

OBJECTIVES

The objectives of this learning activity are to

- ◆ develop an awareness of the root definition of strategic planning

- ◆ describe the various components that are included within a strategic plan

- ◆ share a sample plan (current or former) from the organization, if one is available.

MATERIALS

- ◆ PowerPoint slides 6–10 and 6–11

- ◆ Handout 11–3: Strategic Planning Is . . .

- ◆ Copies of the organization's current or former strategic plan

TIME

- ◆ 20 to 35 minutes, as desired and as session time permits

PREPARATION

- ◆ Review the components of a strategic plan as detailed in Handout 11–3 and slide 6–11 to ensure that the terminology is consistent with that used by the organization. *Vision* and *mission,* for example, may be interpreted differently in the handout or slide than by the organization. Make additional adjustments—such as referring to *core principles* instead of *core values*—as needed to bring the handout and the slide into conformance with the organization's definition and components.

- ◆ If the organization has a current strategic plan or if one is in the process of being revised or updated, make copies for all participants.

INSTRUCTIONS

1. Distribute Handout 11–3 as you display slide 6–10. Explain that the root definition of the word *strategy* (*strategos*) means the "art of the general." Ask participants, *What is the purpose of a general in service to his or her country?* Respondents will typically offer such ideas as *to fight the enemy, to win battles, to win the war, to protect and defend, to plan attacks on the enemy,* and so forth.

2. Explain that the fundamental purpose of a general (and the strategy that the general uses) is less about winning the battle or even the war and more about preserving the empire. Note that generals will often avoid the battle if there are alternative strategies that accomplish the same ends (preserving the empire) without the potential losses and uncertainty of war. Although a general always reserves the option to engage in conflict, it is only one of many strategies.

3. As you display slide 6–11, move from the definition of strategy into the elements of strategic planning. Walk participants through the aspects of this definition. Shift the group's attention to the components of a strategic plan as you reveal the slide line by line.

4. As you gradually introduce the components of a plan, cite pertinent examples from the current strategic plan (if available). Ask participants if they have any questions about these components.

5. Note that the later elements of the plan are really points of transition as the broader strategic plan moves into the daily operational and tactical plans at the unit, subunit, and individual levels.

6. Emphasize that these elements of a strategic plan—even some of the definitions offered here—are not absolute and that each organization can develop its own approach and variation. Suggest that what is most important is that the plan gives people strategic direction in the face of their daily work, an uncertain environment, and a shared aspiration.

7. **Option:** If appropriate and as time permits, refer participants to an abstract or summary of the organization's existing plan. Distribute copies of the abstract of the current plan and ask participants to take five minutes to review the plan at a broad macro level. Ask them to see if they can find each of the components that you have discussed in this activity. After five minutes, ask for comments, reactions, and questions from the group.

DEBRIEFING

At the end of this activity (whether or not you included the optional sharing of the current plan), make these final comments:

- ◆ The fundamental purpose of a plan is to guide people toward thinking and acting strategically.

- ◆ A strategic plan is successful to the extent that it leads to these kinds of outcomes at the individual, unit, and organizational levels.

- ◆ There is no one right way that a plan should look or work. Note that you have highlighted some common components and that some organizations don't include core values in their plan and others merge the vision and mission statements into a single statement of purpose.

- ◆ The plan should reflect the culture and personality of the organization. As a result, the plan that emerges from the strategic-planning process will have a unique identity that may set it apart from other plans developed by other organizations.

- ◆ There is no one right way to plan. Each organization must find its own path.

Learning Activity 11–4: Purpose and Goals of Strategic Planning

OBJECTIVE

The objective of this learning activity is to enable participants to identify the greatest benefits of having a strategic plan for the organization.

MATERIALS

- ◆ PowerPoint slides 6–12 through 6–16

- ◆ Tool 12–6: Selecting Group Leaders

- ◆ Training Instrument 11–3: Why Should We Have a Strategic Plan?

- ◆ Training Instrument 11–4: Purpose and Goals of Strategic Planning

- ◆ Flipchart and marking pens, if desired

TIME

◆ 20 minutes

PREPARATION

◆ If desired, prepare a flipchart page with the question, *Why Have a Strategic Plan?*

INSTRUCTIONS

1. Display the first part of slide 6–12 as you ask participants to tell you the definition of *sanity*. Some people may know the definition. If so, affirm their correct response by revealing the second part of the slide and the definition. Note that one of the key objectives of strategic planning is to achieve *different* results—which means dong things in different ways. We're "insane" when we keep hoping for a different outcome but continue to do things as we have always done them. Strategic planning provides an opportunity to walk in the "sane" lane.

2. Distribute Training Instrument 11–3 as you display slide 6–13. Ask participants to take a minute to jot down some ways a strategic plan might benefit this organization. Give them a minute to do this.

3. Ask everyone to turn to their table partners and take three to four minutes to share the ideas they've written. Invite them to be as specific as possible. (**Option:** If desired, and using suggestions from Tool 12–6, ask each group to select a leader.)

4. Reconvene the group as a whole and ask the small groups to share their ideas about why an organization should have a strategic plan. Record their ideas on the prepared flipchart page, if desired.

5. When most of the reasons have been shared/recorded, distribute Training Instrument 11–4 as you display slides 6–14 and 6–15, and gradually reveal (line by line) the reasons why and how a plan can benefit the organization. Invite participants to fill in the blanks as you share these key reasons.

6. Display slide 6–16, noting that strategic planning is about deciding on which road to travel; it's about making choices and being decisive. It is based on the belief that not just any road will get us where we want to go as an organization.

DEBRIEFING

Conclude the discussion with the following remarks:

◆ The greatest value of a strategic plan is the focus that it gives to an organization and to its leaders and staff at every level.

◆ The plan is productive and constructive to the organization to the extent that it helps people at every level make decisions and take actions.

◆ An effective strategic plan strives to strike a balance between exercising strategic control and encouraging divergent thought and action. Although strategic control helps shape the actions of leaders and staff to ensure an enduring focus on a shared goal, the plan should be open and receptive to new and divergent perspectives and actions. Historically, this is the greatest challenge to strategic planning: bringing focus and direction to everyday thought and actions while giving people permission to explore and discover divergent and innovative opportunities.

Learning Activity 11–5: Value of Strategic Thinking

OBJECTIVES

The objectives of this learning activity are to

◆ define strategic thinking and its role in contributing to the strategic plan and to long-term organizational success

◆ identify the characteristics that enable someone to be a strategic thinker

◆ identify organizational and personal actions for developing and strengthening strategic thinking.

MATERIALS

◆ PowerPoint slides 6–17 through 6–20 (or 8–3 through 8–6, depending on the workshop you're conducting)

◆ Handout 11–4: Strategic Thinking Is . . .

◆ Handout 11–5: Strategic Thinking, Strategy Formulation, and Implementation

- ◆ Handout 11–6: Developing Strategic Thinkers

- ◆ Tool 12–6: Selecting Group Leaders

- ◆ Training Instrument 11–5: Actions to Develop Strategic Thinkers

- ◆ Training Instrument 11–6: Personal Plan for Strategic Thinking

- ◆ Flipchart and marking pens

TIME

- ◆ 35 minutes

PREPARATION

- ◆ If desired, prepare flipchart pages titled *Individual Actions to Develop Strategic Thinkers* and *Organizational Actions to Develop Strategic Thinkers*.

INSTRUCTIONS

1. Move into this activity by reminding participants that the purpose of strategic planning is to create conditions in the organization that support the emergence of strategic thinking. Explain that in this exercise they will turn their attention to better understanding strategic thinking and will begin exploring ways to develop this quality in the organization.

2. Distribute Handout 11–4 as you display slide 6–17/8–3. Note that strategic thinking involves an individual or team integrating the strategic vision/mission and core values into their daily work, paying attention to issues at the edges of the organization, being open to emergent opportunities and threats, and being aware of the interdependencies. Suggest that these qualities are essential to keeping a strategic plan vibrant and responsive to new information and events.

3. Distribute Handout 11–5 as you discuss the various components of the diagram in slide 6–18/8–4. Note that strategic thinking is essential to both the strategic plan and the organization itself.

4. Point out that strategic thinking and the divergent thought that occurs because of it give birth to the strategic plan, shape its development, influence its implementation, and play a key role in keeping the plan relevant to a changing environment and marketplace.

5. Explain that developing competent strategic thinkers is just as important as developing the strategic plan. Indicate that if people are thinking and acting strategically, what the organization actually does within the plan (or even outside of it) is more likely to reflect a thoughtful, long-term, and strategic perspective.

6. Ask participants if they have any questions about strategic thinking and its role in and importance to strategic planning and to the life of the organization itself. As questions emerge, invite others in the group to offer their answers—and then add your own as concluding comments.

7. Move into the next step of this activity by noting that it's not enough to talk about the role and importance of strategic thinking. Organizations need to actively develop strategic thinkers at all levels. Emphasize that every organization needs as many strategic thinkers on the front line as they have in the executive boardroom.

8. Distribute Training Instrument 11–5 as you display slide 6–19/8–5. Ask participants to work in small groups to identify specific actions that individuals and the organization can take to develop strategic thinkers. Ask groups to select a group leader (using one of the selection ideas from Tool 12–6, if desired). Give the groups five minutes for this activity.

9. Reconvene the group as a whole and lead a reporting of ideas for both individual actions and organizational actions. Record groups' ideas on your prepared flipchart pages.

10. Distribute Handout 11–6 and display slide 6–20/8–6 as a summary of some possible actions. Reinforce the ideas offered by the group, noting that theirs are practical steps that they (and the organization) can begin taking tomorrow.

11. **Option:** As time permits, distribute Training Instrument 11–6 and ask participants to identify two or three actions they personally can take to strengthen their own strategic-thinking mindset or that mindset in others.

DEBRIEFING

In your concluding remarks, summarize the following key points:

◆ Strategic thinking is the backbone of long-term organizational success. It should drive both the formulation of the strategic plan and ongoing adjustments to the plan. Strategic thinking keeps the plan—and the daily actions of leaders and staff at every level—responsive to real-world events and conditions.

◆ Long-term organizational success depends on organizational learning—the capacity of the organization continuously to discover new and emerging pathways into an unknowable future by integrating the results of its past actions with the overarching strategic vision of the desired future.

◆ Organizational learning, in turn, depends on people at every level who are able to think and act strategically.

◆ Strategic thinking is key to the success of a strategic plan and all members of the organization must strengthen this quality in themselves and others.

Learning Activity 11–6:
Levels of Planning in Organizations

OBJECTIVES

The objectives of this activity are to

◆ identify the various levels of planning in organizations

◆ involve participants in assessing the amount of time they *currently* spend at each level—and the long-term consequences of staying at the tactical and operational levels to the exclusion of the other levels

◆ involve participants in identifying an *ideal* percentage of time at each planning level and developing a plan to spend more time at the *interactive* and *strategic* levels.

MATERIALS

◆ PowerPoint slides 6–21 through 6–26

◆ Handout 11–7: Strategies for Escaping from the Tactical

◆ Tool 12–6: Selecting Group Leaders

◆ Training Instrument 11–7: Levels of Planning in Organizations

◆ Flipchart and marking pens

TIME

◆ 40 minutes

PREPARATION

◆ If desired, prepare a flipchart page with the heading *Escaping from the Tactical . . .*

INSTRUCTIONS

1. Suggest to participants that although the focus today is on strategic planning, there are other types of planning in every organization. Distribute Training Instrument 11–7 and display slide 6–21 as you highlight the four levels of organizational planning (including strategic planning). Point out that these levels are listed in order from the most reactive and short-term level (tactical) to the most proactive and long-term level (strategic).

2. Discuss the characteristics of each level of planning as you walk the group through the four levels. Give examples of what each level might look like in the organization.

3. Note that during an average month each of us spends a percentage of our time at each of these levels. Suggest that it might be interesting to assess how much time we currently spend at each planning level, how much time we think we *should* be spending at each level, and how not achieving that preferred level of planning may affect one's work and success.

4. Direct participants to the last two columns on slide 6–21. Ask them to assign a percentage to each of the four levels in the *current (C)* column (totaling exactly 100 percent) and in the *desired (D)* column (again, totaling exactly 100 percent). Give them three to four minutes to do this self-assessment.

5. Display slide 6–22 as you ask the participants to discuss in their small groups their current and desired percentages and to answer the questions on the slide. You may want to ask the groups to choose a

group leader, using one of the methods in Tool 12–6. Give the groups 8 to 10 minutes for this activity.

6. Display slide 6–23 and reconvene the large group by asking participants to share how much time in a typical month they currently spend at the tactical or tactical/operational level. (**Note:** It's your choice whether to focus on the tactical or the tactical/operational level.) When individuals have shared their percentages (typically from 55 to 95 percent), ask them to share what the ideal percentages should be for the four planning levels.

7. Some participants may respond to this discussion by suggesting that the percentages will vary according to the respective job level (for example, frontline employees and supervisors will tend to spend most of their time at the tactical and operational levels). Agree with these observations and point out that every organization must spend time effectively planning for and managing both their tactical and operational levels. The real question is *What are the consequences if we work almost exclusively at these two "lower" levels?*

8. Lead a discussion of the consequences for individuals, teams, and the entire organization if the organization's focus remains fixed on these levels. Expect to hear such comments as these: *burnout, high stress, mistakes, no learning from our past, our best people will leave, customer service quality deteriorates, missed opportunities,* and *eventual erosion of the organization's effectiveness, competitive edge, and profitability.*

9. Acknowledge to the group that a lot of good happens at these levels. In many respects this is where real work gets done. It is also, for some people, a place that gives them meaning (as it should). And for some, the frenetic, quasi-crisis mode of action provides an adrenaline rush that, in the short term, yields considerable satisfaction for a job well done.

10. Point out that for the long term, healthy organizations need to find the right balance of these levels. Summarize for the group that there isn't one final list of the ideal percentages across the four levels. At a minimum, individuals should spend 5 to 10 percent at the strategic level. The higher the person is in the organization, the greater the need to spend more time at this level—but strategic planning is not only for this level. Emphasize that it is everyone's responsibility, to varying degrees, to escape from the tactical and to think strategically.

11. Point out that what is most important is that individuals at every level find a way to carve out space for the "upper levels" of planning to ensure the long-term health of the organization.

12. Display slide 6–24 as you ask people to turn back to their small groups and identify specific actions that individuals and the organization can take to enable people to escape from the tactical and to find a more balanced distribution of planning levels. Give groups five to seven minutes to identify at least three specific actions or steps people can take individually or organizationally to bring more strategic thinking into tactical and operational levels.

13. Reconvene the large group and ask people to share their ideas for escaping from the tactical. At the conclusion of the activity, display slide 6–25 and distribute Handout 11–7. The slide lists and the handout explains some ideas to help people make this escape.

DEBRIEFING

◆ Explain that the tactical and operational levels are the lifeblood of every organization. Your success as a manager, supervisor, or staff member is defined by how well you deliver results for the organization and its customers at these two levels.

◆ Note that the challenge for most of us is to prevent these two levels from dominating our work lives. Finding methods for integrating the interactive and the strategic with the operational and tactical is the key to long-term success for the organization.

◆ Display the Henry David Thoreau quote on slide 6–26. Emphasize that working hard just isn't good enough—what matters is working hard for the goal. Thoreau reminds us that all of the activity at the tactical and operation levels must remain anchored to the vision and the higher purpose that the vision represents.

◆ Conclude the activity by encouraging participants to integrate the lessons learned and the list of possible individual and organizational actions into their daily practice.

Learning Activity 11–7:
An Integrated Model for Strategic Planning

OBJECTIVES

The objectives of this activity are to

- ◆ introduce a model for strategic planning that integrates the insights from the four levels of organizational planning

- ◆ enable participants to see the relationship between strategic planning and the other planning levels within an integrated framework that translates the strategic plan into daily work.

MATERIALS

- ◆ PowerPoint slide 6–27

- ◆ Handout 11–8: An Integrated Strategic-Planning Model

- ◆ Flipchart and marking pens, if desired

TIME

- ◆ 15 minutes

PREPARATION

- ◆ You may want to have the "Parking Lot" (Tool 12–5) ready as a place to post questions concerning the integrated model and how it will work in the organization that can't be answered during the workshop.

INSTRUCTIONS

1. Display slide 6–27 and distribute Handout 11–8 as you direct participants to focus on an integrated strategic-planning model. Note the two "spheres" of action: The lower sphere represents the realm of strategy formation. In this realm those involved in the strategic-planning process work together to create the strategy to guide the organization into the future.

2. Point out the key outcomes from this strategic-planning realm of action (vision, mission, core values, and strategic issues). Indicate that *how* these aspects of the strategic plan are formulated depends on the approach to strategic planning taken by the leadership or strategic-

planning team. Indicate that the different approaches to strategy formulation will be covered in the workshop on advanced issues (which some of the participants may be attending).

3. Emphasize that strategy formation is more a creative and intuitive process than a rational/analytical one. Point out that although gathering and analyzing data from the internal and external environments is a key to strategy formulation, at the end of the day what emerges is a collective sense of where the organization needs to be (the shared vision and mission) and how (its core strategies) it should move toward that vision.

4. Whether strategy formulation involves an extensive competitive analysis, an exploration of alternative scenarios, or the identification of distinctive "core competencies," the development of strategy is typically more intuitive than pure reason and rationality.

5. Indicate that later in this workshop—and in the advanced issues workshop—you will explore some approaches to strategy formulation. For now, however, shift attention to the upper sphere—the realm of strategy implementation.

6. Point out the link between the lower or strategic sphere and the upper or operational sphere. It is in this upper sphere that the plan moves into the heart and soul of the organization, where the strategic plan translates into everyday work. Highlight the fact that it is in this realm that interactive, operational, and tactical planning come into being. These "where-the-rubber-meets-the-road" planning processes direct and guide daily work throughout the organization.

7. Note that this operational level is where the reality of the strategic plan unfolds. As results and outcomes are realized or missed, the insights that emerge from this level can and must be integrated into the plan. Call attention to the feedback loop that involves making adjustments and revisions to the plan based on emerging issues and the results or effects of the organization's daily actions.

8. As time permits, ask participants to work in small groups and discuss the integrated model. Invite them to develop at least one question about the model that they'd like some information on. Give the groups about three minutes for this buzz-group activity.

9. Reconvene the large group and ask for questions. Encourage participants to answer their own questions as much as possible. Offer your

own responses as appropriate. Highlight those questions that may not be easily answered today (especially those relating to making the plan operational) and write them on the "Parking Lot" flipchart page.

DEBRIEFING

Make the following summary comments as you guide participants in integrating this activity and developing their personal action plan:

♦ Although this integrated model is less prescriptive than the "planning school" diagram displayed earlier, it still requires a thoughtful step-by-step methodology to help ensure that the vision and strategic goals effectively translate into action and results.

♦ Strategic thinking at the operational and tactical levels is very important because it enables people to recognize strategic opportunities and subsequently change what they are doing or what they should do in the future.

♦ The purpose of a strategic plan is to shape the way people think and act in their daily work. The integrated strategic-planning process outlined here demonstrates how this influence and guidance can and should be felt at every level of the enterprise.

Learning Activity 11–8:
Stages of Strategic Plan Development

OBJECTIVES

The objectives of this activity are to

♦ enable participants to apply the four stages of developing a strategic plan to their own organization

♦ guide participants in identifying specific actions that they can take at each planning stage to develop an effective strategic plan.

MATERIALS

♦ PowerPoint slides 6–28 through 6–34

♦ Handout 11–9: Actions for Each Strategic-Planning Stage

♦ Tool 12–6: Selecting Group Leaders

◆ Training Instrument 11–8: Stages of the Strategic-Plan Development Process

◆ Flipchart and marking pens, if desired

TIME

◆ 60 minutes

PREPARATION

◆ If the organization's leaders or strategic-planning committee have a specific set of actions they believe should occur at each stage and they want to share these actions with participants, either add the information to Handout 11–9 or prepare a separate handout.

INSTRUCTIONS

1. Display slide 6–28, noting that strategic planning involves making choices and pursuing those choices with focus and energy. The alternative—chance and waiting—moves you out of the driver's seat and puts fate and hope in charge. This is not enough to enable the organization to achieve its goals.

2. Shift attention to the new activity (the stages of developing a strategic plan) by displaying slide 6–29. Gradually reveal the four stages of developing a strategic plan as you provide a quick summary of each stage.

3. Indicate that developing a plan requires intuition and a sense of what needs to happen (based on good data from the environment), as well as a rational, step-by-step process for translating the vision and strategic issues into daily operations.

4. Distribute Handout 11–9 and display slide 6–30 as you explain that specific actions, methods, and processes need to be implemented at each stage of plan development. Say that you will be asking them to work in their small groups to identify some ways to accomplish the specific desired outcomes at each stage.

5. Distribute Training Instrument 11–8 and draw everyone's attention to the first page. Note that there is a series of questions that the first stage of the process must answer for a strategic plan to take shape.

State that their goal for the next 10 minutes is to identify the specific actions, methods, steps, processes, and so forth that must happen to accomplish the objective of this stage.

6. Assign one stage of the process to each small group. If you have more than four groups, assign the same stage to more than one group. Ask groups to select group leaders (drawing on ideas in Tool 12–6) to guide them in the process of identifying specific methods and actions that the organization's strategic planning team would need to take to answer the questions in the left-hand column. Tell them that they will have 10 minutes to formulate answers and that they will be expected to report their ideas to the large group.

7. Emphasize that the purpose of this activity is not actually to answer the questions or to develop the beginnings of a strategic plan. Rather, the present goal is to identify *how* to accomplish the key tasks of each stage to enable the development of a strong and effective strategic plan. Give people 10 minutes for this activity.

8. Give small groups a three-minute warning, letting them know that they should be prepared to report their ideas and strategies for accomplishing the tasks of each step.

9. Guide each group in reporting their recommended actions. Encourage participants to make notes on their respective pages of Training Instrument 11–8 so they capture some of the ideas from the groups.

10. Stress the links between the stages and how they work together to construct a plan. After each of the groups reports its recommended actions for each stage, follow up by displaying the appropriate slide (6–31 through 6–34) that lists your ideas for action. Tell the participants that you will be sharing with them the ideas on the slides in a handout at the end of the activity.

11. As the groups report and you add your own suggestions to theirs, sketch out the four stages of the strategic-plan development process on a blank flipchart page. Build the drawing sequentially, adding each stage to the diagram after the groups have reported their ideas. (See figure 11–1 for an idea of what this diagram might look like after you've facilitated a discussion of the four stages.)

As you diagram the four stages, point out the gap between the current reality (stage 1) and the desired future (stage 2) and how this gap is closed by the strategic issues that emerge during stage 3. Point out that stage 4 is represented on the diagram in the detailed operational plans that are created by the key strategic issues.

12. When all the groups have shared their ideas, tell participants that some organizations choose to flip the order of the first two stages. They prefer to identify the shared vision and then conduct the environmental scan and gather data about the present. Suggest that this is a matter of personal style and preference by those leading the planning process. Each order has its advantages and disadvantages.

13. Point out that where plans typically fall apart (something that is explored in a later learning activity) is in the transition from a statement of aspiration and goals (the strategic vision) to the operational details of who does what. Explain that if these last details (who is responsible, how success will be measured, how changes are made to the plan, and so forth) are not directly addressed, the plan will fail.

Figure 11–1
The Four-Stage Strategic-Planning Process

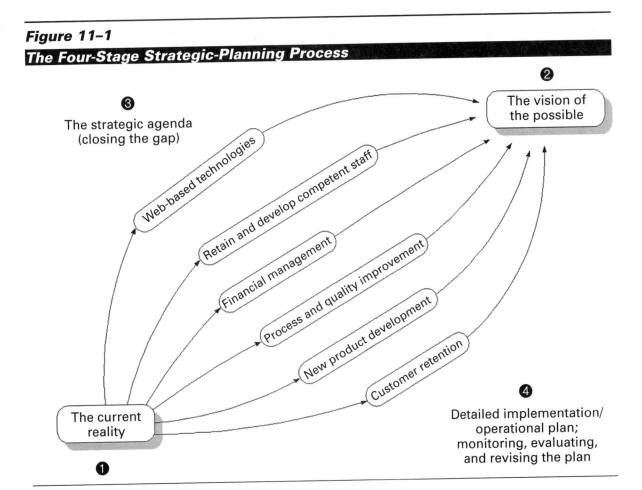

❸ The strategic agenda (closing the gap)

❷ The vision of the possible

Web-based technologies

Retain and develop competent staff

Financial management

Process and quality improvement

New product development

Customer retention

❶ The current reality

❹ Detailed implementation/ operational plan; monitoring, evaluating, and revising the plan

DEBRIEFING

◆ Highlight the importance of this four-stage process in developing a high-quality strategic plan. Note that the process that the organization follows is just as important as the final plan that results. The quality of the plan depends on good data and good people asking good questions.

◆ Emphasize that there is no one right way to develop a strategic plan. Suggest the right way is the one that works, the one that prepares the organization for the future and gives it guidance in facing the challenges ahead.

◆ Remind participants that the key challenge to this process is successfully making the leap from an inspirational declaration of the kind of organization you want to be to making all of that happen in the midst of (and perhaps in spite of) the chaos and confusion of the operational and tactical world.

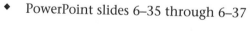

Learning Activity 11–9: Involving Stakeholders in the Strategic-Planning Process

OBJECTIVES

The objectives of this activity are to

◆ identify the key stakeholders who should be involved in formulating and sustaining the plan

◆ guide participants in identifying various methods for involving key stakeholders.

MATERIALS

◆ PowerPoint slides 6–35 through 6–37

◆ Training Instrument 11–9: Who Develops the Strategic Plan?

◆ Training Instrument 11–10: Personal Plan for Strategic Involvement

◆ Flipchart and marking pens

TIME

◆ 45 minutes

PREPARATION

- You may want to modify Training Instrument 11–9 to reflect the diverse stakeholder groups that are likely participants in the strategic-planning process.

- Prepare two flipchart pages, each divided into two columns. In the left column, drawn more narrowly than the right column and titled *Stakeholder*, you will name the key stakeholders identified by the group. In the right column, titled *Involvement Ideas*, you will write participants' specific suggestions for involving those stakeholders.

- Review Training Instrument 11–10 and decide if you will use it in this activity.

INSTRUCTIONS

1. Display slide 6–35 and ask participants to answer the question *Who should develop the strategic plan?* Guide the large group discussion, inviting people to question and challenge the answers that emerge from this discussion.

2. Point out in your summary comments from this question that there are several critical points in the four stages of plan development when ideas and insights from stakeholders other than the executive leadership team are essential to the relevancy and vitality of the plan. Suggest that although the entire organization doesn't develop the plan document (this is best done by a selected group of people who bring a sharp strategic and systems focus to their efforts), every level of the organization must be engaged in its development to some degree.

3. Display slide 6–36 and distribute Training Instrument 11–9. Ask participants to work in small groups to (a) identify the five stakeholder groups that are most critical for involvement in the development of the strategic plan; (b) identify at least two or three specific opportunities for involving each of these key stakeholder groups; and (c) decide how the strategic-plan development process should be designed to accommodate and integrate the data, information, and insights from these stakeholders. Ask participants to select a group leader to keep the group on task during the activity and tell them they have 10 minutes to accomplish these three tasks.

4. Reconvene the full class. First invite the groups to identify their top five stakeholder groups. Write all of the stakeholder groups in the left-hand column of the flipchart page, spacing the groups listed to allow filling in examples of involvement in the right-hand column and using the second prepared page if needed. When all of the key stakeholder groups have been identified, go back to the beginning of your flipchart list of stakeholders and start filling in the right-hand column. When ideas for involvement are offered, ask for examples and as many specifics as possible to ensure there is clarity in *how* each group should be engaged and involved in the process.

5. Encourage an active discussion of these strategies for involvement. Offer your observations on the value of participation versus consensus.

6. Highlight the importance of an integrating team that takes the lead in actually developing the plan. If the organization has already appointed such a team, point out the members of the team, the team's title, and their formal role in developing the strategic plan.

7. Emphasize that this team doesn't create the strategy as much as it tries to bring to the surface the key strategic opportunities and challenges facing the organization—bringing awareness to all levels of the organization. Note that a formal strategic plan will emerge to guide daily operational and tactical planning—but that how the plan is developed, who is involved in its development, and how they are involved can make all the difference in engaging the organization.

8. Point out the important role that these stakeholders play *after* the plan is developed to ensure that the plan is operationalized at the department/work-unit level and that it continues to stay relevant through continuous review and renewal.

9. **Option:** As time permits, distribute Training Instrument 11–10 and invite participants to identify some actions they can take to ensure that their perspectives and insights contribute to the emerging strategic plan. Encourage them to think about how they can contribute their ideas and what they individually can do to encourage the active contributions of others from their departments, work areas, or teams. After four to five minutes, invite them to pair up with someone at their table or an adjacent table and share their personal involvement ideas. Encourage them to use their partners as sounding boards to fine-tune their personal involvement strategy.

DEBRIEFING

♦ Display slide 6–37. Ask participants what Deming's quote means in the context of this discussion of involvement. Agree with comments offered that suggest that a strategic plan is only effective to the extent that it encourages people to say what needs to be said—to tell the truth. Agree also that if stakeholders tell the truth, the plan will more closely reflect the issues that need to be addressed to move the organization successfully into the future.

♦ Make the point that by now it's obvious that an effective strategic plan reflects the insights and perspectives of more than just a few people at the top of the organization. Suggest that this learning activity sought to refute the notion that strategic planning is for the executives to create and for the rest of us to implement.

♦ Highlight the importance of leadership in formulating strategy and making the key strategic choices (for example, establishing the strategic vision, selecting the long-range goals, entering new markets, shifting focus from low-cost to high-value provider).

♦ Emphasize that the CEO and executive leadership team still are the final decision makers who set the strategic direction—but that if these leaders fail to involve and engage other stakeholders at every level of the organization (and outside of it), their "executive decisions" may be grounded in incomplete data and the opportunity to learn from the tactical and operational levels of the organization will be lost.

Learning Activity 11–10: Organizational Strengths to Support and Sustain Strategic-Plan Implementation

OBJECTIVES

The objectives of this activity are to

♦ identify what the organization currently does right that demonstrates its capacities to implement and sustain the strategic plan

♦ guide participants in identifying specific actions that they can take to strengthen successful strategic-plan implementation

◆ enable participants to use these strengths to address some common obstacles to implementation.

MATERIALS

◆ PowerPoint slides 6–38 through 6–40

◆ Handout 11–10: Common Obstacles to Developing and Implementing a Strategic Plan

◆ Training Instrument 11–11: Organizational Strengths to Support and Sustain the Strategic Plan

◆ Training Instrument 11–12: Actions to Address Potential Obstacles

◆ Flipchart and marking pens

TIME

◆ 45 minutes

PREPARATION

◆ Prepare two flipchart pages, titled *Organizational Strengths Supporting the Strategic Plan* and *Actions to Address Obstacles and Support Implementation.*

INSTRUCTIONS

1. The background to this activity lies in the discipline of AI, which is explained in detail in chapter 3. The premise of AI is that every organization has a reservoir of talents and strengths that it can draw on to accomplish difficult and challenging tasks. This activity focuses on the strengths of the organization in the areas of strategy creation and development, strategy implementation, goal setting, and operational implementation. So instead of focusing exclusively on what could go wrong with strategic-plan development and implementation (obstacles and barriers), this lesson begins with participants identifying what the organization does well in these areas. Once identified, these strengths will serve as the foundation for addressing potential obstacles to strategy implementation.

2. Introduce the activity by suggesting to participants that successfully developing and implementing a strategic plan is a complex and diffi-

cult task. It requires diverse stakeholders coming to agreement on a shared vision; integrating insights about the organization's past and the current and emerging environments; making complex strategic choices regarding future directions and goals; developing detailed strategic implementation plans that require organizational commitments and actions to move the organization forward; and blending these plans with existing organizational commitments, actions, and operations.

3. Explain that this complexity will require the organization—at every level—to draw on its competencies and strengths as it works to create a meaningful strategic plan that moves the organization toward its strategic goals. Display slide 6–38 that essentially asks *What competencies and strengths do we have as an organization that will enable us to successfully develop and implement a meaningful strategic plan?*

4. Distribute Training Instrument 11–11 and ask the small groups to take the next 10 minutes and answer the questions on the training instrument that explore their perceptions of the competencies, strengths, and successful track record that can serve as a reminder of what the organization can do when it puts its mind to it. Ask the groups to select leaders and be prepared to report their responses to the whole class.

5. Reconvene the large group and facilitate a discussion of those organizational competencies and strengths that demonstrate that a positive and meaningful plan will emerge from the planning process. Record the groups' responses on the prepared flipchart page.

6. Take time to celebrate the list of competencies and strengths, and urge participants to work in their own way to translate these organizational strengths into an effective strategic plan supported by strong and diverse strategic thinkers throughout the organization. Indicate that you will transcribe their list of organizational strengths and distribute the list to each of them as a way to reinforce the capabilities and positive track record of the organization.

Note: Some groups may have difficulty coming up with competencies and strengths, preferring to talk about what the organization *doesn't* do well. Before responding too quickly to these concerns, explore what other groups have discovered in their discussions. If other groups have a similar problem, refocus the talk of inadequacies toward competencies by shifting attention to even the small things that the organization does well. Identify a beginning point for building an effective capability for strategic planning.

7. Distribute Handout 11–10 as you note that there are some common obstacles to strategic-plan development and implementation of which every organization should be mindful. Gradually reveal the key points on slide 6–39, allowing time for people to fill in the blanks as you move through the topic.

8. Distribute Training Instrument 11–12 and display slide 6–40 as you ask the small groups to return to their discussion, this time identifying how the organization's strengths can help address some of the common barriers identified in Handout 11–10. Give the groups seven or eight minutes for this buzz-group activity.

9. Ask the groups to report their recommended actions. Record their ideas on the prepared flipchart page.

DEBRIEFING

◆ Emphasize that an organization develops an effective strategic plan by first understanding its strengths and competencies.

◆ Note that strategic thinking is a fundamental competency that helps support the development and implementation of a strategic plan. Point out that strategic thinking by everyone in the organization helps ensure that the right issues are brought to the surface and that the plan evolves over time as people at all levels share insights, lessons, and issues emerging at the tactical level.

◆ Remind everyone that they, individually, are key to the successful development and implementation of the strategic plan. Although the executive leadership or strategic-planning team may have the primary responsibility for crafting the language and making the strategic choices, the health and vitality of the plan depend on the continuing engagement of people at every organizational level. Suggest that, among the organization's many strengths, they are by far the most important

Learning Activity 11–11: Characteristics of an Inspiring Vision for the Future

OBJECTIVES

The objectives of this activity are to

- enable participants to describe the role and importance of creating an inspiring vision

- identify the characteristics of an inspiring and compelling vision.

MATERIALS

- PowerPoint slides 7–4 through 7–7

- Handout 11–11: The Role and Power of an Organization's Shared Vision

- Handout 11–12: Characteristics of an Inspiring Vision

- Handout 11–13: Sample Vision Statements

- Flipchart and marking pens

TIME

- 25 minutes

PREPARATION

- If the organization has a vision or mission statement, decide if the statement will be shared with the group and whether the group will be asked to assess/evaluate the statement.

- Prepare a flipchart page titled *Characteristics of an Inspiring Vision.*

INSTRUCTIONS

1. Ask the large group how many years it took to build the great cathedrals of Europe. You can expect to hear a range of responses from a dozen years to several hundred. Agree with the higher numbers, suggesting that many of these great cathedrals took centuries to construct—and some remain unfinished. For example, Notre Dame in Paris took 300 year to complete; London's Westminster Abbey about

500 years; the cathedral in Strasbourg, France, more than 200 years; and Salisbury Cathedral in Great Britain 38 years. With this as a context, tell the following story of the three stonemasons.

Stonemasons Story

Centuries ago there was a traveler walking across what is today France. This traveler came to an open area where hundreds of workers were busy laboring in the hot sun. The traveler approached one of the workers and asked him what he was doing. The man, all caked with a mixture of dirt and sweat, turned toward the traveler and, with an irritated scowl, said "Can't you see, I'm laying stone!"

The traveler quickly backed away, excusing himself. Still curious, however, he approached another of the men laboring in the heat of the day. "Excuse me. Can you tell me what you're doing here?" This second man, bending into his work, barely turning his head toward the traveler, grunted "Can't you see, I'm building a wall!" And then he too ignored the nosy visitor.

But our traveler was still curious. In his last attempt to find out the purpose of the men's work, he approached a third man. He asked again, "My good fellow, can you tell me what you're doing here in this field?" The man turned to face the traveler. He too was struggling with the heavy stone in the sweltering heat. He was covered from head to foot with the fine dust that hung heavy in the air. His face was streaked with sweat, but as he turned the traveler could see a fire in his eyes; a spark of energy that was absent in the eyes of the other two men. "I'm building a great cathedral," the third man said. "A monument to God!"

Now it was clear that this third man would never live to see the inside of his great cathedral. He would never hear the sacred music rise and echo off its fan-vaulted ceilings. He would never view the brilliant glow of the sunlight filtering through stained-glass high above the altar. In fact, it's likely that even this man's great-great-grandson—also destined to be a stonemason—wouldn't live to see the cathedral completed. And yet, this stonemason's vision of his great "monument to God" carried him forward. It elevated his effort. It transformed his difficult work into something greater than him.

2. Move from the story into the next part of the activity by suggesting that the story exactly captures the purpose of a vision: to elevate our thoughts toward something greater than ourselves and to engage the

individual and collective spirits of the organization. Explain that, although our own vision statements may deal with more earthly matters, the vision we create should strive to capture our imaginations and focus our energies.

3. Distribute Handout 11–11 and display slide 7–4 as you describe the role that vision plays in moving the organization away from its current state (and its proud traditions) toward a compelling alternative future.

4. Suggest that the more compelling a vision is, the more it carries the power to pull the organization toward a desired future. Point out the creative tension that the vision seeks to prompt—a tension that emerges when the vision pulls the organization away from the present.

5. Note the role that tradition and the status quo sometimes play in tugging in the opposite direction. Point out that although the organization can embrace its proud past and its traditions and that there may be much in the status quo that is positive, the capacity to grow and the ability to move in a new direction depend on a powerful vision. Explain that the vision must challenge complacency and status quo thinking—and even the organization's past successes—to catalyze the thinking and actions of organizational stakeholders.

6. Explain the elastic relationship among the vision, the present, and the organization's past. Point out that as the vision pulls the present forward, the organization's traditions and successful past aren't forgotten but are carried along behind.

7. Display slide 7–5 and ask the large group to name the characteristics that enable a vision to be inspiring to employees. If desired, record the group's ideas on the prepared flipchart page.

8. Display slide 7–6 as you distribute Handout 11–12. Gradually reveal the characteristics on the slide, allowing time for participants to fill in the blanks where appropriate. Stress that a vision's significance is not in what it says or how it looks hanging on a banner in the office; it's in what the vision *does:* inspires people to think and act in a profoundly different way.

9. Distribute Handout 11–13 and ask participants to take the next five minutes as a group to discuss the sample vision statements included there and to offer their thoughts in response to the questions on slide 7–7.

10. Next facilitate a brief discussion of the groups' reactions to the sample vision statements. Emphasize that what matters most is not what *we* think of these vision statements, but what *employees* in these companies think about them. If the statements work for the employees, if the statements elevate daily work, if they provide inspiration or guidance, if they help employees connect to something larger than themselves, then the vision statements have done their jobs.

11. **Option:** As time permits (or as you have designed it), share the organization's current vision statement and ask participants to take five minutes with their small groups to discuss the vision. Encourage them not to get specific about what they like and don't like in the statement, but rather to see if the vision gives them a sense of a higher purpose and cause for their work. After five minutes, reconvene the larger group and ask for small-group reports.

DEBRIEFING

◆ Stress that creating a *shared* vision is a key component to formulating strategy and developing a strategic plan.

◆ Note that visions are hot items these days so special care must be taken to ensure that a vision truly is a clear statement of the organization's core purpose—one that gives it meaning and focus and captures people's imagination.

Learning Activity 11–12: Creating a Shared Vision for the Future

OBJECTIVES

The objectives of this activity are to

◆ model a process that participants can use to create a shared vision for their department/work area or to contribute to the organization-wide vision

◆ identify vision themes based on participants' own aspirations that can be used as part of the organization's strategic-planning process.

MATERIALS

- ◆ PowerPoint slide 7–8

- ◆ Writing paper for participant use during the activity

- ◆ Flipchart, easel, and markers of various colors for each small group

TIME

- ◆ 60 minutes

PREPARATION

- ◆ Put a small stack of writing paper on each table.

- ◆ Place flipchart easels around the periphery of the room so that each small group will have access to an easel when needed.

- ◆ Prepare a flipchart page titled *Vision Themes*.

INSTRUCTIONS

Note: This activity typically follows Learning Activity 11–11, which discusses the vision and its role in the strategic plan and in the organization.

1. Move the group from discussing the context and nature of the shared vision, as explored in Learning Activity 11–11, to beginning the development of this vision. Indicate that you will lead them through one approach to a visioning process that they can use in developing a shared vision beyond today's workshop.

2. Tell participants that you are going to issue a challenge to them. Read them the following four paragraphs:

   I want you to imagine that through the magic of time travel, this room and everyone in it has been catapulted 10 years into the future. Imagine that in this future time you walk out of the room and through the halls of the organization. As you take a tour, you talk with employees, managers, and leaders. There is an energy in the air that is hard to describe. People are acting, interacting, and moving forward in ways you have never seen before. You see and hear great things happening! To your amazement, in this future much of what the organization had set out to accomplish years ago was actually realized!

You step outside the organization and interact with customers, suppliers, and other business partners. And you visit the surrounding community. Great things have been accomplished by the organization for these customers, business partners, and even the larger community. There has been a significant change—a profoundly positive change—that explains how different the organization is now from the way it was a decade ago.

You realize, sadly, that it's time to return to the past (today!). But, before you return, you want to capture and share what you have observed, witnessed, and experienced. You decide to send a postcard back to the time you came from (the present year). Take a minute right now and write that postcard before you forget what you've seen and experienced. Make sure that you jot down special accomplishments, what it felt like, who the organization served, what difference it was making in people's lives, the kinds of people contributing to the vision, and so forth.

Because the best postcards are picture postcards, make sure you draw a picture of something you observed. Perhaps there is a symbol or singular image that stands out about this future place. Whatever visuals you saw, try to capture those as well in your postcard from the future.

3. Give participants five or six minutes to work by themselves. Gently discourage interaction or talking while encouraging deep reflection on what it was like to visit the organization 10 years from now. While everyone works, move the flipchart easels into position beside each table.

4. Gauge your time by reading the group for visual cues of readiness and tell participants that it's time for them to share their postcards from the future with their small-group partners. Before they begin, instruct the groups to pay attention to the themes that emerge and to record on the flipcharts beside their tables key themes, images, stories, and the like when everyone has spoken. Ask the members of each small group to take turns sharing their postcards. Encourage them to have fun with their reports and encourage listeners to ask questions and explore more about what the authors saw in the future. Allow 10 minutes for this exercise.

5. Display slide 7–8 as you challenge the small groups to shift toward creating a flipchart page that defines and describes the shared vision that emerged from the postcard stories. Encourage them to use visuals—color, symbols, images—to paint a vivid picture of the organiza-

tion's ideal 10 years from now. State that they will then be asked to present their vision, images, and stories to the whole group. Encourage them to use poetry, rap, a song, a skit—anything they think will help them express the power and inspiration of their vision. Give them 15 minutes to work in small groups.

6. Reconvene the large group and ask for volunteers to share group vision descriptions in colorful ways. Be energetic and reinforce an upbeat and positive environment. As the individual groups finish their vision presentations, lead the applause to keep the energy level high. Watch your time to allow an opportunity for all of the groups to report.

7. Ask participants to identify key themes that they heard across the groups. Record these on a flipchart page.

DEBRIEFING

◆ Note that the vision doesn't have to be something terribly complex or difficult. It must, however, tap into the creative energy and spirit of those who are key stakeholders in the organization's success.

◆ Indicate that the great ideas that sprang from the vision statements in this activity won't be lost because the flipchart pages and vision themes will be saved and shared with the group and used within the strategic-planning process.

Learning Activity 11–13: Defining Core Values

OBJECTIVES

The objectives of this activity are to

◆ describe the role that core values play in a strategic plan and its implementation

◆ demonstrate a method for identifying core values as part of a strategic-planning process.

MATERIALS

◆ PowerPoint slides 7–9 through 7–12

◆ Handout 11–14: Characteristics of Core Values

◆ Handout 11–15: Sample Core Values

◆ Training Instrument 11–13: Discovering Core Values

◆ Flipchart, easel, and marking pen for each table

TIME

◆ 35 minutes

PREPARATION

◆ If the organization has a current set of core values or principles, make a copy for each participant.

◆ Place flipcharts on easels around the periphery of the room so they can easily be moved into position beside each table when needed.

◆ Prepare a flipchart page titled *Our Core Values*.

INSTRUCTIONS

1. Make the point that a strategic plan has three major components: the vision/mission, the strategic agenda, and the core values. Emphasize that all three are essential to guiding the organization toward its desired future, but core values may most directly influence the individuals' daily work.

2. Suggest that whereas the vision speaks to the heart and the strategic issues speak to the head (for example, by enumerating an employee's goals for the next quarter), the core values speak to the hands, feet, and mouth. The core values are the guiding principles that shape employees' daily behaviors. They give direction on how to resolve a conflict with a customer, how to solve a difficult problem, how to make a tough decision, and so forth.

3. Point out that if the core values are widely understood and embraced, they can assist and support the emergence of strategic thinking because it puts the power of strategic PSDM in the hands of those on the front line.

4. Distribute Handout 11–14 and display slide 7–9, both of which present the characteristics of effective core values. Lead the class through the characteristics. Respond to any questions on the role and function of core values in the strategic plan and the organization.

5. Distribute Handout 11–15 and display slide 7–10. Explain that the handout lists the core values of a number of organizations. Point out that most of the statements are clear and specific. By focusing on only a few core values, these organizations make very apparent what they stand for, what they expect, and how people at every level should conduct themselves.

6. Distribute Training Instrument 11–13 and display slide 7–11. Ask participants to work on their own, following the instructions on the instrument, and finally to settle on their three most important personal values. Ask them to work quickly. Give them about five minutes to make their decisions.

7. While they work, move the flipchart easels into position beside each table.

8. Display slide 7–12. Ask participants to share their top-three value lists with the other members of their small groups. Instruct groups to use their flipcharts to record the members' values and then select the top four or five key value themes that emerge. Discourage them from getting too analytical about the sifting process or focusing too much on the language of their top core values. Encourage them to talk about what the values mean to them and then, out of these discussions, to choose the group's top four or five core values. Give the groups about 10 minutes for sharing and choosing.

9. After the small-group discussion, ask groups to report their top core values. When all have done so, ask the whole class to suggest or identify key core value themes that emerged during the reporting.

10. If desired, record these summary core values on the prepared flipchart page and say that you will be sharing this summary of core values with those who are leading/guiding the strategic-planning process for the organization.

11. **Option:** As time permit, ask the provocative question, *Can core values be counterproductive to the organization?* If someone says "yes," ask for examples of how and when core values can lead to undesirable results. If no one else does so, point out that the downside of strong core values is that they may exert too much control over individual behavior and thus stifle creativity, innovation, risk taking, and serendipitous discovery. Suggest that as powerful and productive as

core values can be in guiding people toward desired behaviors, they also can lead to narrow-minded thinking and acting and therefore undercut the very purpose of strategic thinking.

Point out that culture (which is one way in which core values are expressed) plays a powerful role in shaping everyday behavior. Encourage participants to harness the power of culture and values, but also to recognize when the core values exert more control and power over daily decision making and action than might be desirable.

DEBRIEFING

◆ Stress that core values are the primary points of contact between the strategic plan and each employee. Whereas the vision describes the desired destination and the strategic agenda identifies the specific steps the organization will take to get there, the core values give direction to every moment, every interaction, every situation, everyday for every staff member.

◆ If you have discussed the downside to core values, remind them that these values can be counterproductive and that employees should be watchful to ensure that the values serve the strategic long-term interests of the organization and the employee and do not simply act as ways to control employee behavior.

Learning Activity 11–14: Conducting a SWOT Analysis

OBJECTIVES

The objectives of this activity are to

◆ discuss the importance of an environmental scan—a SWOT analysis—as part of the strategic-planning process

◆ demonstrate one approach for conducting a SWOT analysis

◆ gather participant perspectives on the key environmental challenges and opportunities facing the organization. (As an additional benefit of this activity, the organization's leadership or strategic-planning team can integrate these perspectives into the planning process if they wish.)

MATERIALS

- PowerPoint slides 7–13 through 7–18

- Handout 11–16: The SWOT Analysis: Understanding the Organization's Environment

- Four wallcharts (each 4 x 6 feet)

- 3 x 3-inch sticky-notes and fine-point, felt-tip pens (one pad and pen for each person)

- Flipcharts, easels, and marking pens

TIME

- 50 minutes

PREPARATION

- If, by necessity, there are more than 24 to 26 participants, you may need to adjust the process to accommodate the additional people during the SWOT sorting phase of the activity.

- Place flipcharts around the periphery of the room so they can be moved easily into position at each table when needed. Ensure that the easels don't impede sight lines during the large-group discussion segments of the activity.

- Hang the four wallcharts around the room, labeling each with their respective SWOT titles: *Strengths, Weaknesses, Opportunities, Threats.* You can use butcher paper, rolls of newsprint, or multiple flipchart pages taped together to create these wallcharts.

- Prepare one flipchart page by labeling it *Our Internal Environment.* Under the title, list some key internal organizational systems: *communications, teamwork, operations, fulfillment, leadership, supervision, performance management, decision making,* and *quality improvement.* Hang the page on the wall at the front of the room.

- Prepare one flipchart page labeled *The External Environment.* Under the title, list some key forces outside of the organization: *social, political, economic, technological, cultural,* and *demographic.* Hang the page on the wall at the front of the room.

- On the tables, place pads of sticky-notes and pens for each person.

INSTRUCTIONS

Note: This activity is designed to facilitate a SWOT analysis for a single organization for which all of the participants work. If this is not the case, simply note that participants should answer the questions for their own organizations—and that the class will see if there are environmental trends that surface across all of the organizations represented. Note that, although such cross-organizational scans (particularly the internal environmental aspects) are less useful for identifying the environment for a specific organization, participants will learn the methodology for conducting a SWOT analysis.

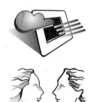

1. Display slide 7–13 and ask participants to partner with someone at their tables or a neighboring table and discuss the question that you have displayed there. Give them three to four minutes to discuss their thoughts and perspectives.

2. Reconvene the large group and ask for some examples of the significant forces shaping the organization and its future. When people have offered several of these forces, ask the large group how the organization should go about identifying these forces; how it should capture the ideas that they listed; and how it should integrate such issues into a strategic plan.

3. Respond to the ideas offered by the group by indicating that all models and approaches to strategic planning have some provision for considering and integrating an *environmental scan*. Explain that an environmental scan is designed to help the organization identify the forces internal and external to itself. On the basis of the resulting broader awareness of the world in which the organization operates, it can then pull together a plan that incorporates this awareness of the surrounding and emerging environments.

4. Distribute Handout 11–16 and display slide 7–14 as you describe the four perspectives on the environment—the SWOT analysis.

5. Emphasize that the review of the surrounding environment is often done within the context of the organization's vision statement. Remind participants of the current or emerging vision statement (elements of which may have been identified in an earlier activity) and ask them to think about that vision of the future as they consider the four environmental dimensions.

6. Indicate that, first individually and then as a group, they will explore the four dimensions. Ask individuals to pick up one sticky-note pad and a pen.

7. Explain the "rules" for using the sticky-notes for this activity: When presented with a question, each person should print his or her answers on separate notes. They should use short, clear, headline-style responses because others will eventually need to be able to read their notes. As you describe the process, model it for the group, showing them how to work quickly and how to make a stack of notes for each of the four questions. Ask if the instructions are understood and answer any queries.

8. Tell participants that they will now consider the first of the four SWOT dimensions: organizational strengths. Display slide 7–15 and refer to the prepared flipchart page labeled *Our Internal Environment*. Direct participants to consider the various organizational systems listed there as they answer the first question. Tell them to work quickly to identify as many answers to the question you are about to ask as they can, and remind them to write each answer on a separate note. Suggest they reread the list of systems on the flipchart page to ensure that they consider all aspects of the organization's internal environment. Tell them they have three to four minutes to work silently and independently.

9. Ask the first question, *What are the strengths of our organization?*

10. Call time and ask them to put an identifying sticky-note on the top of the first stack of answers—*Strengths*.

11. Tell participants it's time to turn their thoughts to the second SWOT dimension: organizational weaknesses or areas for improvement.

12. Refer again to the *Our Internal Environment* list as you display slide 7–16. Instruct everyone to produce as many sticky-note answers as they can in three to four minutes and ask the second question: *What are the weaknesses or areas for improvement in our organization?*

13. Call time and ask them to place a title note on top of the second stack.

14. Walk toward the flipchart page labeled *Our External Environment* as you display slide 7–17, and guide them through the first of the two external environment considerations: opportunities.

15. Tell them they will now have three to four minutes to create a stack of answers to the third question: *What are the opportunities available to our organization?*

16. Call time and remind them to place a title note on the top of the third stack of answers.

17. Display slide 7–18 and give them a brief explanation of the fourth SWOT dimension: threats. Remind them to consider the list of external factors on the flipchart page at the front of the room as they take three to four minutes to answer the last question.

18. Ask the fourth question: *What are the potential threats to our organization?*

19. Call time and ask them to label their fourth stack of answers.

20. Bring the group's attention back to the front of the room and explain the next steps in the SWOT process:

a. Point out the four wallcharts, each labeled with one of the four SWOT dimensions. Indicate that the next step of the process is to have everyone place each of their sticky-notes on the wallchart representing each note's respective SWOT dimension. Explain that all you want them to do is put their notes on the appropriate chart without paying any attention to order or structure. Instruct them to move quickly now, to place the notes in their four stacks on the appropriate wallcharts, and to return to their tables.

b. Now demonstrate the next step—organizing the notes into related or similar groupings. Approach one of the charts and move related notes around, reading them as you do so to show that you are moving similar notes together and making related groups or categories (as yet unnamed). Make only a few moves.

c. When you've completed the demonstration, tell them it's their turn to do the same thing. Tell them that this step of the process is done *SILENTLY*. They are not to talk with one another during the activity. They are to move the notes around on the charts without discussing the notes or the emerging categories. Explain that when disagreements arise about where a note belongs, they are to resolve the disagreement without discussing it. Give them permission to create new notes if necessary.

d. Explain that they will have seven to eight minutes to sort the notes into five to seven groupings or categories. Stress the importance of five to seven categories: fewer than this means they likely have grouped together things that should be separated; more than this means they may have broken a single issue into too many subparts. Ask for and answer any questions about the process.

e. Either assign groups to specific charts or allow them to go to the chart of their choice—with no more than eight people at a chart. Instruct them to wait until you tell them to begin the sorting.

f. Tell them to start, and gently remind them of the need for silence during this activity. Give a two-minute warning to speed everyone along. Encourage them to do their best to find a home for each note.

g. Call time and tell people to remain at the charts. Say that the next step of the process is to discuss categories that have naturally emerged and then draw a border around each category and label it with another note or by writing on the chart. **Note:** Tell participants *not* to use their marking pens for writing on the charts because the ink will bleed through the paper onto the wall!

h. Give the groups at the charts seven to eight minutes to discuss their categories, define the boundaries of each category, and label each category. Ask them to return to their tables when they have completed the grouping and labeling.

21. Ask participants to comment on the *process* that was used to develop the categories for each SWOT dimension. Point out that the technique is called *affinity diagramming*—a powerful PSDM tool that enables a group to identify issues and trends without extended discussion and debate.

22. Quickly highlight some of the major groupings on each of the four wallcharts. As you note the groupings for each SWOT dimension, point out that everyone should be thinking about which issues are most important to include and address within the strategic plan.

23. Note that these results will be used in the next step of the strategic-planning process: selecting the internal and external environmental forces and factors that are likely to have the greatest impact on the future success of the organization.

DEBRIEFING

♦ Stress that understanding the environment is critically important to creating a relevant and successful strategic plan.

♦ Note that the SWOT analysis often is done within the strategic-planning process after the vision has been clearly defined. With the vision in mind, participants in the SWOT analysis explore the environment for forces that are most likely to influence or affect the achievement of the vision.

♦ Emphasize that the results of this process will be strongly influenced by who participates. Suggest that the goal is to have as much of the whole system as possible in the room at one time when identifying these issues. Failure to include a perspective or insight can lead to an eclipsed sense of the internal and external environments.

♦ Indicate that if the size of the group makes it impossible to have key voices from the larger system represented and participating in identifying the environmental forces, some other mechanism (for example, surveys or focus groups) should be used to capture and represent the insights of others in the affinity diagramming process.

Learning Activity 11–15: Defining the Strategic Agenda

Note: In most cases, this activity should follow Learning Activities 11–12 and 11–14, in which the group identified some preliminary elements of the organization's vision and conducted the SWOT analysis. SWOT wallcharts should be posted in the room.

OBJECTIVES

The objectives of this activity are to

♦ explain how to develop the strategic agenda—the key strategic issues that define the core elements of the strategic plan

♦ introduce the "balanced scorecard" and other approaches for selecting a broad strategy for achieving the vision.

MATERIALS

- PowerPoint slides 7–19 through 7–21

- Handout 11–17: Selecting the Strategic Agenda

- Colored half-inch sticky-dots (one red and four green dots for each participant)

- Flipchart and marking pens

TIME

- 45 minutes

PREPARATION

- Find out if the organization's leadership or strategic-planning team has chosen an overarching approach or method for deciding the strategic agenda and plan to use that approach in this activity. If the approach chosen is one of those described in Handout 11–17, be certain to point that out. If it isn't, either create a handout that incorporates the approach or replace the first steps of the activity with a discussion of the chosen approach.

- Prepare a flipchart page that displays the stages of the strategic-planning process (see figure 11–1, p. 139).

- Place groups of dots at each seat around the tables.

INSTRUCTIONS

1. Introduce the activity by approaching the prepared flipchart page and indicating that a strategic plan tries to define at least three key factors: the current state (the present), the desired state (the vision), and the strategies to move from the current to the desired state (the strategic agenda). Explain that this activity explores ways to identify the strategic agenda—ways to choose the five to seven core strategies that will take the organization toward its ideal.

2. Display slide 7–19 and distribute Handout 11–17. Read aloud the two questions on the slide and then give participants five minutes to read about the various approaches presented in the handout.

3. Display slide 7–20 and tell participants to discuss in their small groups the different approaches to developing the strategic agenda and to follow the directions contained on the slide. Ask the groups to select a group leader to guide the discussions and to be prepared to report their responses and questions. Give them eight minutes for the group work.

4. Reconvene the large group and facilitate a discussion of the different approaches or methods for developing the strategic agenda. Give examples and respond to questions as they surface. Encourage participants to answer the questions posed by other groups.

5. Make a transition to the next segment of the activity by noting that when selecting the issues to include in the agenda it is important to consider which issues are likely to have the greatest impact on the organization's ability to achieve its vision.

6. Display slide 7–21 and define *high leverage.* Note the importance of this principle. Explain that there may be dozens of actions that the organization could take to make progress toward its vision and that the key choice to make when selecting strategies is to choose actions that are likely to bring the greatest gain for the organization. Give an example of where high leverage can be an effective way to move a large object/organization.

7. Ask the participants to keep both the elements from the organization's vision (gleaned from Learning Activity 11–12, if appropriate and desired) and the idea of high leverage in mind as you lead them through one way of integrating the vision and high leverage into a method for guiding the selection of the key strategic issues.

8. Explain that over the next five minutes you'd like them to hold the ideal vision of the organization's future in mind, to think of the principle of high leverage, and to review the array of SWOT issue groupings identified in Learning Activity 11–14 and posted on wallcharts. (If time permits, it may be useful to highlight the major groupings from the SWOT analysis.) Explain that each person will vote for five issue categories among all of those on the wallcharts that he or she believes are the most important ones for achieving the organization's vision and that should be included in the strategic agenda.

9. Point out the red and green dots at each place and explain that they'll use these dots to cast their votes. Tell them that the red dot is

the *most powerful* of their five votes. It counts twice as much as the green dots. So when they vote they should cast the red-dot vote for the most important of the five issue categories. Ask for and answer any questions about the dot-voting process, and encourage them to work quickly.

Note: If participants ask why someone would vote for a strength or for an external opportunity, explain that strengths represent competencies that should be preserved and continued (and therefore deserve a vote) and opportunities need to be prepared for and taken advantage of. In most cases such opportunities don't just fall into our laps; we need to work at making sure we are able to capitalize on them.

10. Instruct participants to move to the wallcharts and to place their dots within the boundary lines of an issue category. Explain that they can spread their votes out in any way they wish—there is no need to place a dot on every SWOT chart. Tell them they have five minutes and instruct them to begin.

11. Give a two-minute warning to speed up those who are still considering their votes.

12. Call time. Point out clear trends in the voting. Highlight those categories that received the most votes. Calculate the vote totals (red dots count 2 points each; green dots 1 point) and highlight those that received the highest vote totals. Within the border of each category, record the number of votes and circle the number of points.

13. Ask for reactions from the group (reactions to the sticky-dot voting process as well as to the final results).

14. Point out that the issue categories that received the most points are ones that the organization should include at some level of its strategic agenda. Note that the agenda may include other issues that relate to their competition, the CEO's or other leaders' priorities, and so forth, but that the primary issues identified here should be addressed in some way.

DEBRIEFING

◆ Stress that the process used today to select the strategic agenda is only part of a larger discussion at the leadership level for setting the strategic agenda. Reiterate, however, that the ideas that surface from the SWOT analysis and voting must be considered when deciding on the strategic issues that become part of the strategic plan.

◆ Note that deciding on the core strategic agenda—that which the organization decides to undertake to move it toward its vision—is a critical choice. When an issue gets placed on the agenda, it receives attention, energy, support, and commitment. And, when an issue isn't on the agenda, it may lose these things. For this reason, the selection process should be thoughtful, deliberative, and certainly strategic.

◆ Emphasize that the strategic agenda should and will change as new environmental issues and factors emerge, as conditions and markets change. Explain that this is the nature of organizational life, but stress that the initial strategic agenda is a beginning that gets the plan moving forward.

Learning Activity 11–16: Developing Strategic Action Plans

OBJECTIVE

The objective of this learning activity is to provide participants with an action-planning template they can use to create the detailed plan that moves the organization from an abstract idea to actions and behavior at all levels.

MATERIALS

◆ PowerPoint slides 7–22 and 7–23

◆ Handout 11–18: Template for Strategic Action Planning

◆ Handout 11–19: Sample Strategic Action Plan

◆ Flipchart pages and markers, if desired

TIME

◆ 35 minutes

PREPARATION

◆ Revise Handouts 11–18 and 11–19 to reflect the organization's intended or actual practice of action planning as part of the strategic plan.

INSTRUCTIONS

1. Begin the activity by noting that all great strategic visions and plans eventually have to come down to people thinking and acting in new ways to move the organization in new directions. In such a context, the challenge for any strategic plan is to catalyze new behaviors throughout the organization and in specific areas.

2. For every great dream, ambitious goal, or grand conception, we have to find a way to make it happen. One way is just to urge people to work harder, think differently, or work smarter. Another, more focused way is to develop a detailed plan that specifies what needs to happen, when it needs to happen, how it will be accomplished, who will do the work, and how the results will be measured.

3. Acknowledge that not everything can easily be translated into a detailed plan. But note that for most issues on the strategic agenda, developing a detailed plan that identifies what the organization will do and how it will measure its success is fundamental to moving forward.

4. Distribute Handout 11–18. Describe this template as one approach to developing the detailed action plan to move a strategic issue forward. Acknowledge that this simple template can't capture all of the complexity involved in addressing a strategic agenda item, but suggest that the template can be used as the framework for developing a more detailed and intricate action plan.

5. Suggest, for example, that a high-level action plan could be developed with this template to chart the overall direction of the organization's efforts and a subset of supporting action plans could be written to develop the detailed work of individual teams, departments, and work areas for specific aspects of the larger action plan. In this sense the proposed action-planning template can be replicated at multiple levels in support of the larger strategic agenda.

6. Highlight the major sections of the action plan by displaying slide 7–22. Ask for and answer questions as you review the structure of the action plan.

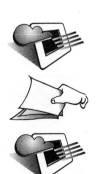

7. Distribute Handout 11–19. Ask participants to read through the sample plan. After five minutes, display slide7–23 and ask the small groups to answer the questions on the slide. Give the groups six or seven minutes for discussion.

8. Reconvene the large group and invite a discussion of the action-planning template. Discuss issues, reservations, and questions that have arisen. Encourage the large group to answer the questions that are posed.

9. Again acknowledge that this is only *one* approach. There are other action-planning tools that may include more or fewer steps or issues. Encourage people to offer ideas to strengthen the organizational effectiveness of this action-planning tool. Record these ideas on a flipchart, if desired.

DEBRIEFING

◆ Emphasize that every strategic plan needs a formal mechanism to move the organization closer to its strategic objectives and vision.

◆ Point out that this action-planning template or some variation must be used if the organization is to shake off old patterns and pathways and move in a new direction.

◆ Thank everyone for offering tool-improvement suggestions and note that their suggestions will be incorporated into the final planning documents used to guide the organization's strategic-planning efforts.

Learning Activity 11–17: Implementing the Strategic Plan in the Face of Uncertainty and Chaos

OBJECTIVES

The objectives of this learning activity are to

◆ remind participants of the uncertainties of organizational life and enable them to see the necessity of the strategic plan being open to emergent issues

◆ guide participants in developing a personal plan for dealing effectively with uncertainty and emerging issues that challenge the strategic plan.

MATERIALS

◆ PowerPoint slides 7–24 through 7–27

◆ Handout 11–20: Lessons from Chaos and Complexity Theories

◆ Training Instrument 11–14: Personal Action Plan for the Lessons from Chaos and Complexity Theories

◆ Flipchart, easel, and marking pen for each table

TIME

◆ 45 minutes

PREPARATION

◆ Place flipcharts on easels around the periphery of the room so they can easily be moved into position beside each table when needed.

◆ Identify some additional examples of unplanned events that demonstrate how uncertainty and emergent issues can affect plans and intentions.

INSTRUCTIONS

1. Display slide 7–24 and ask, *What is the relationship between the adhesive qualities of duct tape and presidential legacy?*

2. You will likely get some puzzled looks and perhaps a few laughs. Expect that no one will suggest the connection right away. If no one offers a guess, give a few hints: *early 1970s, the Watergate Hotel, and the "Plumbers."*

3. By this time there will usually be someone in the room who will know the answer: *the break-in at the headquarters of the Democratic National Committee (DNC) at Washington's Watergate building on the night of June 17, 1972*—an event that turned out to be a key precursor to the downfall of the Nixon presidency.

4. Tell the whole story:

   The night janitor was walking down a hallway in the office building connected to the Watergate Hotel, checking doors to ensure that all were locked. He found that one door—the door to the DNC—had duct tape over the latch. Assuming that people had been moving boxes or furniture out of the offices earlier and had simply forgotten to remove the tape, he removed the tape, checked that the door was locked, and continued down the hall. Some time later that night he noticed that the door was taped again and immediately called police . . . and the rest is history. The revelation of the burglary of the Democratic Na-

tional Committee headquarters began unraveling the Nixon presidency (he resigned from office on August 9, 1974) and significantly affected Nixon's presidential legacy.

Remind participants that life is filled with unseen and unplanned events that profoundly influence what's on our plates tomorrow. A serendipitous unexpected discovery of a lock taped open had enormous consequences for a man and a nation.

5. Ask participants if they have similar examples of unplanned events or incidents that led to profound social, political, or economic changes to a business, community, or some other entity. Offer more examples to strengthen the insight that, frequently, the best-laid plans fall by the wayside in the face of emergent issues.

6. Emphasize that an uncertain world doesn't render our planning obsolete; it just requires us to find creative ways to sustain movement toward the vision—or, perhaps, to modify our vision in the face of new information.

7. Note that despite our efforts to impose order and structure on an organization through strategic, operational, and tactical planning, things happen and things change in the real world. Sometimes our plans succeed; sometimes they fail. Our strategies must make room for emergent issues while we do our best to stay true to our vision.

8. Display slide 7–25 and distribute Handout 11–20 as you explain that chaos and complexity theories—two theories from the new sciences —give us some important insights into the "natural order" of the universe—a universe that very clearly includes organizations.

9. Explain that chaos and complexity theories argue that the rational/ analytical world we attempt to create in organizations is partly an artificial one. In the natural world—in *complex adaptive systems*, to use one term from these theories—living systems are always changing and reacting to unfolding events while following their natural pathway toward simply "being."

10. Explain that Handout 11–20 offers some "lessons" from chaos and complexity theories and might be useful as the organization develops and implements its plans. These theories also may help the organization build a key capacity of all healthy living systems: learning. Learning involves strategic thinking, openness to the environment and to serendipity, awareness of wholeness and connections among the parts, and the capacity to change future behavior based on what we are discovering now.

11. Ask participants to read the handout as you display slide 7–26. Direct them to identify for themselves the implications of these principles for strategic planning. Ask them, as well, to identify which principles might be most useful in helping the organization develop, implement, and (perhaps most important) sustain a vital and effective strategic plan. Give them five or six minutes to read the handout and reflect on the slide's two questions.

12. Instruct them to share their thoughts with the members of their small groups, and ask groups to identify specific actions that individuals and the organization can take to integrate the lessons from these theories into the strategic-plan development process. Ask them to record individual and organizational actions on their flipcharts. Give the groups 15 minutes for their discussions.

13. Reconvene the large group and facilitate a discussion of the implications of chaos and complexity theories in how the organization approaches strategic planning. Ask each group to share its specific actions (individual and organizational) for ensuring that the strategic-planning process benefits from the insights from chaos and complexity theories.

14. Following that discussion, distribute Training Instrument 11–14. Ask participants to spend the next four or five minutes identifying—perhaps from the ideas generated from the group discussions—personal actions that they can take to promote the integration of these theories into the strategic-planning process—or into their personal approach to strategic thinking, planning, and acting. Give them five minutes to do this.

15. Ask them to pair up with another person and share their intended actions. Encourage partners to offer feedback and suggest additional approaches to one another.

DEBRIEFING

◆ Acknowledge that our plans for the future are repeatedly challenged by the unforeseen and unexpected circumstances in the real world.

Explain that strategic planning is no different. In fact, by its nature it is more subject to the vagaries of the real and unpredictable world than are even our tactical- or operational-planning efforts.

◆ Explain that our response to this uncertainty is not to abandon our planning efforts but to stay true to the vision and make adjustments in our daily practice to accommodate the uncertainties of everyday life.

◆ Note that the challenge that uncertainty presents for us is to preserve the integrity of our vision—our overarching goal—while we maintain our flexibility in how we attain the goal.

Learning Activity 11–18: Developing the Strategic Issues Map

OBJECTIVES

The objectives of this learning activity are to

◆ develop strategic-thinking skills

◆ infuse strategic-thinking insights into the current organizational environment.

MATERIALS

◆ PowerPoint slides 8–7 through 8–9

◆ Handout 11–21: Exploring the Strategic Issues Map

◆ Training Instrument 11–15: Implications and Actions from the Strategic Issues Map

◆ Training Instrument 11–16: Personal Plan for Strategic Thinking from the Strategic Issues Map

◆ Copy of the organization's vision or mission statements, if available

◆ Wallchart prepared as specified in the activity

◆ Three colored markers, one each in red, blue, and green

TIME

◆ 2 hours, 10 minutes

PREPARATION

- ◆ Arrange the training room so that participants will be able to work in small groups for the first part of the learning activity and then in a half-circle facing the wallchart for the second part of the activity.

- ◆ Prepare a wallchart of the Strategic Issues Map. See figure 11–2.

- ◆ If available, write out the organization's vision and/or mission statements on flipchart paper and post near the Strategic Issues Map.

Figure 11–2
Strategic Issues Map

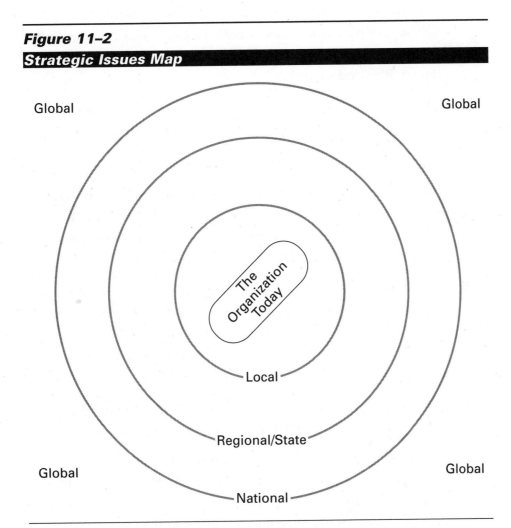

Note: You may want a more organic, flowing design for this map. If so, don't create concentric circles. Just place the organization's name in the center of your chart. When you use the map in your workshop, ask participants to list local issues first. When those have all been written in closest to the name of the organization, make some sort of unobtrusive boundary mark and ask them to identify the regional/state issues, and after that the national issues, and then the global issues. Don't feel compelled to constrain your creativity.

◆ Prepare a flipchart page titled *Forces* that lists the following bullet points: *social, political, economic, technological, cultural,* and *demographic.* Post this flipchart page near the Strategic Issues Map.

INSTRUCTIONS

1. Display slide 8–7 and begin the activity with the question, *Why is strategic thinking just as important as strategic planning?* Invite participants to respond with their ideas. Given that this learning activity won't typically be the first exposure to the concept of strategic thinking, participants will likely offer such answers as *good strategic planning depends first on good strategic thinking, strategic thinking is what matters most in day-to-day decision making, strategic thinking helps people look for and find emerging issues that may not be addressed by a strategic plan,* and so forth.

2. Make it clear that you're not saying that strategic planning isn't important—it is crucial. Explain that because strategic *thinking* is the foundation of what we do in the present and it shapes the direction of our future work (through planning), it undergirds our planning and must be a central competency that organizations develop. Because people on the front line often see and hear things that top executives never see or hear, frontline workers at every level must develop strategic-thinking skills.

3. Indicate that this activity focuses on enhancing individual and collective awareness of the environment in which the organization operates. By fine-tuning this awareness and by emphasizing the importance of *action* based on it, individual and collective strategic-thinking skills will grow.

4. Shift the group's focus to the wallchart. Ask participants to leave their tables and take chairs in the semicircle facing the chart.

5. Point out the organization's vision/mission statement (if you've posted it near the chart). Note that the vision/mission statement describes the organization's core purpose—what it strives to create for customers, the community (perhaps), the world (perhaps), stakeholders, shareholders, and employees. The vision represents what the organization hopes to achieve through its work.

Note: If the vision/mission is in the process of being revised as part of the strategic plan, acknowledge this and note that the vision is evolving and may change as various pieces of the strategic plan come together.

6. Ask participants to hold this vision in their minds as they reflect on the questions you will be posing to them over the next hour or so. Indicate that one of the key ingredients to effective strategic thinking is having the vision and what it means clearly in mind as one approaches a task.

7. Direct participants' attention to the center of the wallchart. Note that, because the organization as it is today is the focus of our Strategic Issues Map, it is identified at the center of the map. Suggest that, over the next 30 minutes or so, you will be writing down some of the key issues that they identify as influencing the organization today and in the near future.

8. If you've created your map as a series of circles, point out that the concentric circles surrounding the organization at the center reflect the relative distance from the organization: local, regional/state, national, and (outside the circles) global. If you have opted for a more organic design for your map, explain the relative distance of issues in whatever way makes sense with your design. Simply indicate that you will move from the center outward—thinking first locally, then regionally, then nationally, and finally globally.

9. Also call attention to the *Forces* flipchart page posted near the wallchart. Note that, as participants respond to the questions you pose, they should reflect on these forces and factors as possible origins of some of the strategic issues that they identify.

10. Indicate that, starting with the local circle, you would like people to offer what they see as some events, trends, and issues currently influencing the organization or likely to influence it in the future. Note that these events can be either positive or negative—you're not talking only about the obstacles to the organization's success but also about things that will positively influence its future.

Ask people to offer ideas occurring at this level even if they aren't sure that there is an influence on the organization or its future. Tell them that the goal is to fill the map with issues and events that they are seeing or experiencing even if the effect or influence on the organization isn't clear.

11. As people offer ideas, write them quickly and clearly within the "local" area. Further stratify the forces and factors by asking contributors of ideas if the local items are closer or farther from the organization.

    Note: The local area should be filled with information about what is happening now and in the recent past. These issues are perhaps the best known by participants, so give sufficient time and space for the issues to be plotted. Don't worry, for now, about the relationship among events and trends. You'll sort this out later on.

12. As you record information in the "local" area, periodically remind everyone to think of the vision statement and of local issues that might facilitate or impede the organization moving closer to that vision. Continue working in the "local" area until the group goes silent. (Expect to spend about 10 minutes recording the local events.) Indicate that they can add other local events later if they occur to them later.

13. Shift the group's attention to "regional/state" forces and factors. Follow the same process for recording events, reminding participants of the vision and forces flipchart pages. Continue to add issues, events, and trends that people report on the regional level. As with the local issues area, point out that they should offer ideas even when they aren't sure if there is an impact on the organization today or in the near future.

14. After you have guided the group through the regional/state area, shift its attention to the national area. Emphasize that in this area they should think of the forces, events, and issues that are occurring and are influencing the organization today or are likely to in the months and year ahead. Note that although the distance from the organization may be greater, there likely is a wide array of national issues that will have an influence on the organization. Remind the group of the vision statement and the posted forces list to ensure that everyone considers these elements as they identify issues and events.

15. Finish your primary mapping activity by guiding the group through the "global" realm. Here ask them to think of events and issues that are occurring anywhere in the cosmos that might have some current or future influence on the organization. Again, highlight the vision and forces flipchart pages. Acknowledge that these global issues may seem very remote and disconnected, but that it's important to look beyond what is closest to us.

16. When the group has identified the global issues, invite people to offer any local, regional, state, or national ideas/issues that now occur to them—especially ones that may be related to the more distant issues they've identified. Add these to the Strategic Issues Map as they are offered by the group.

See figure 11–3 for an example of what your (concentric-circles) map may look like at this stage of the mapping exercise.

17. Ask the group for its general reactions to what they see sketched out before them. What impressions do they gain from seeing all of these issues and events—many of them directly influencing the organization today and continuing to do so in the future.

Note: At this point the group is likely to be ready for a break. As they leave the room, ask them to reflect further on what they learned in developing the Strategic Issues Map, and tell them to return to the semicircle after the break.

18. Move the group into the next mapping stage: developing the connections and relationships among and between the events, issues, and trends that they have identified.

19. Distribute Handout 11–21 and ask participants the key questions presented there.

When participants identify issues potentially moving closer to the organization, circle those issues with a RED marker. This indicates issues that they need to watch for or pay attention to now.

Next to or on top of forces or issues that are identified as fading, draw a BLUE question mark. Those forces may have a waning influence within the map.

When participants identify drivers, circle them with the BLUE marker. Then draw GREEN lines as arrows stretching between the drivers and the other events and issues that they drive. The point of drawing these lines is to begin sketching the interrelationships among the various events, issues, and trends. The map can get messy at this stage, so do your best to get some consensus before plotting any relationship. Also, when connecting a driver to that which it drives, ask if the arrow is really going the right way. Challenge the group to question some of the causation arrows they have identified.

Figure 11–3

Sample Concentric-Circles Strategic Issues Map

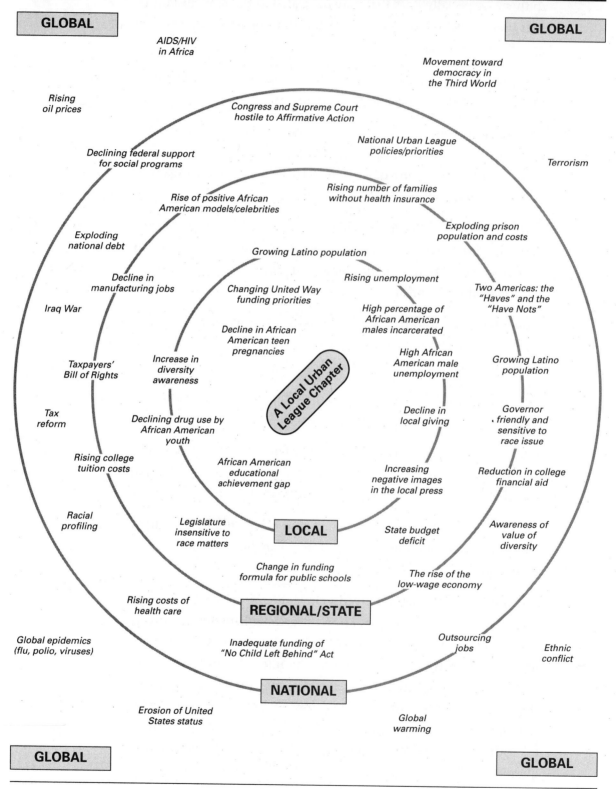

20. When the map has been completed, ask again for general reactions and comments. Offer your own observations on the insights suggested by the group. Point out that in very little time they have sketched out some fundamental issues with implications for the organization and the work of every person there.

21. Ask participants to return to their small groups. Distribute Training Instrument 11–15 and display slide 8–8. Instruct groups to answer the questions on the slide and write their answers on the instrument, keeping the Strategic Issues Map in view as they work. Ask them to choose a group leader who will lead the discussion. Give the groups 10 to 15 minutes to complete their work.

22. Reconvene the full class and ask for groups' answers to the questions. Encourage individuals to note other groups' answers on their sheets.

23. After all of the questions are answered, indicate that it's time to shift back to what each person can do individually, based on the insights from the Strategic Issues Map. Distribute Training Instrument 11–16, display slide 8–9, and ask people to work by themselves to complete this personal plan for translating strategic thinking into action. Give people four to five minutes to do so.

24. As time permits, have participants pair up and take several minutes to share their personal plans and to gather additional action ideas.

DEBRIEFING

◆ Reiterate that the long-term success of any organization is embedded not in the strategic plan but in the hearts, minds, and finally the actions of individuals alone and in concert with others on behalf of the organization.

◆ Remind them that the best way to empower the individual and the organization is to develop strategic-thinking skills. Note that this involves understanding the vision and mission (the organization's core purpose) and the rich and diverse environment in which it functions.

◆ Point out that strategic thinking is powerful in the extent to which individuals translate the insights they gain from the Strategic Issues Map and what they are learning from the environment into strategic *action* that supports the organization's long-term health and vitality.

◆ If appropriate, promise that the results from their Strategic Issues Map work will be combined with the work done in other workshops and integrated into the strategic plan. It will also be shared with the executive leadership team to enable them to see and learn from people at all levels of the organization.

Learning Activity 11–19: Definitions and Distinctions

OBJECTIVE

The objective of this short learning activity is to present some simple definitions of a *problem* and a *decision,* and to highlight distinctions between the two.

MATERIALS

◆ PowerPoint slides 9–8 through 9–10

◆ Training Instrument 11–17: Definitions of a Problem and a Decision

◆ Flipchart and marking pens, if desired

TIME

◆ 10 minutes

INSTRUCTIONS

1. Display slide 9–8 and ask the two questions on this slide as you distribute Training Instrument 11–17. Encourage participants to answer the questions on the instrument and, after a few minutes, share with the large group their thoughts about the differences between these two concepts.

2. After participants have offered their thoughts, find a way to link what some have offered as you display slides 9–9 and 9–10 and reveal the two definitions.

3. Note that a key difference between the two is that decision making involves *choice* among alternatives and that it can also involve pur-

suing an aspiration—not just deciding how to fix something. Note that decision making is one step in solving a problem because it requires sorting out the best way or choice for solving a problem.

4. Emphasize that decision making, however, is not only driven by a problem—it is also driven by aspirations and hope—the desire to move in a new direction and the need to find the best way (choice) to do so.

DEBRIEFING

Conclude this brief activity by emphasizing the importance of being clear in our definitions. Understanding what a problem is, what a decision is, and how they differ from and relate to one another will be useful in learning methods for addressing each.

Learning Activity 11–20: Exploring Our PSDM History

OBJECTIVES

The objectives of this learning activity are to

- identify the individual and collective history with PSDM in the organization to better understand what does and doesn't work with the organization's approach to PSDM

- gain an appreciation of the organization's PSDM strengths and where it could improve

- identify the consequences of both effective and ineffective PSDM.

MATERIALS

- PowerPoint slides 9–11 and 9–12

- Training Instrument 11–18: Exploring Your PSDM History

- Flipchart pages and marking pens

TIME

- 25 minutes

PREPARATION

◆ Prepare two flipchart pages, each divided in half vertically. On one page, title the left column *Why Effective?* and the right column *Consequences*. On the other page, title the left column *Why Ineffective?* and the right column *Consequences*.

INSTRUCTIONS

1. Display slide 9–11 as you distribute Training Instrument 11–18. Ask participants first to work by themselves to think of two specific PSDM situations in which they were involved: one in which PSDM went well and one in which it didn't. Instruct them to describe the situations in the spaces provided on the instrument and to explain what caused it to go well or poorly. Finally, tell them to describe both situations' consequences for the organization. Give them three minutes to do this.

2. Call time and ask participants to choose a leader for each small group and then share their examples, the reasons why PSDM worked and why it didn't, and the consequences of each situation. Display slide 9–12 and read through the instructions they are to follow in their small groups. Give them 10 minutes to complete the activity.

3. Reconvene the large group and ask each group leader to share one reason why PSDM worked/went well and the consequences for the organization. Record these on the *Why Effective?* flipchart page.

4. Ask each group leader to report one reason why PSDM didn't go well and the consequences for the organization and for individuals. Record these responses on the other flipchart page.

DEBRIEFING

◆ Point out that understanding what the organization currently does well in PSDM and where it falters is helpful in strengthening PSDM skills.

◆ Highlight some significant consequences of successful PSDM (for example, *it feels right, we deliver on a promise, we achieve our goal, people feel connected, we actually solve the problem, the problem goes away, people are confident in the decision made, there is no second-guessing*).

◆ Point out significant consequences of poor PSDM (for example, *we deliver poor customer service, opportunities are missed, resources are wasted, there is deepened cynicism, we come up with the wrong answer or solve the wrong problem, the problem only gets worse, we lose good people*). Stress that such consequences make doing it right all the more important.

◆ Highlight some of the common themes—both positive and negative—that emerge in the organization's history with PSDM. Ask participants to pay attention to the methods and tools that you'll be exploring in the workshop as possible ways to avoid PSDM missteps or ways to strengthen PSDM successes.

Learning Activity 11–21: Principles to Guide Strategic PSDM

OBJECTIVES

The objectives of this learning activity are to

◆ identify a set of core PSDM principles to guide participants as they solve problems and make decisions

◆ assess the extent to which the organization practices these principles in its PSDM

◆ identify actions that individuals and the organization can take to improve the application of these principles to everyday PSDM.

MATERIALS

◆ PowerPoint slides 9–13 through 9–15

◆ Handout 11–22: Seven "Breakthrough-Principles" to Guide Strategic PSDM

◆ Flipchart pages and markers, if desired

TIME

◆ 25 minutes

INSTRUCTIONS

1. Suggest to participants that effective *strategic* PSDM involves solving problems and making decisions within a thoughtful framework to ensure the most successful result. Indicate that this framework is best captured as a set of guiding principles.

2. Distribute Handout 11–22 as you display slide 9–13. Indicate that these principles are modeled closely on the work of Gerald Nadler and Shozo Hibino and formed the basis of their book *Breakthrough Thinking.* Those authors believe the principles should guide how people approach every problem they encounter and every decision they make.

3. Display slide 9–14 and ask participants to read Handout 11–22 and identify, in their view, which principles the organization tends to practice more than others—and which principles it tends not to practice. Give them four minutes to review the principles on their own.

4. Show slide 9–15 and direct participants to share with the members of their small groups their thoughts on which principles the organization practices and which it doesn't practice. Ask them to identify specific actions that they personally could take to ensure that less-used principles are applied in the future. Give the groups seven or eight minutes for this discussion. Encourage them to select a group leader—perhaps using some of the selection ideas in Tool 12–6.

5. Reconvene the large group and lead a discussion about the organization's use of the principles. Ask group leaders to report possible actions suggested in their groups to increase the application of less-used principles.

DEBRIEFING

◆ Point out that PSDM occurs all of the time in organizations—it's often not done strategically or in the right frame of mind. Reiterate that the seven principles on Handout 11–22 offer important insights into how to approach PSDM from a more strategic and thoughtful perspective.

◆ Emphasize that these principles help make PSDM *strategic* by ensuring a mindset that is anchored to the vision (principle 2), reflects a long-term perspective (principles 2, 3, and 7), and uses systems thinking (principle 3) to acknowledge the interdependence of each PSDM situation with other organizational problems or decisions that need to be made.

♦ Encourage participants to read the book *Breakthrough Thinking* (Nadler and Hibino 1990) to explore the principles further and to learn more about integrating them into their daily problem-solving practice.

♦ Explain that improving the organization's ability to make its PSDM more effective and strategic depends on individuals (sometimes acting alone) bringing the principles forward in their minds and in their practices.

Learning Activity 11–22: Approaches to PSDM

OBJECTIVES

The objectives of this learning activity are to

♦ identify the two broad approaches to problem solving and decision making

♦ highlight the advantages and disadvantages of each approach and enable participants to know when to use each.

MATERIALS

♦ PowerPoint slides 9–16 and 9–17

♦ Training Instrument 11–19: Approaches to PSDM

♦ Flipchart pages and markers, if desired

TIME

♦ 25 minutes

INSTRUCTIONS

1. Move into this activity by pointing out that there is no one right way to approach PSDM. Suggest rather that there are two broad approaches—each appropriate in its own way and in its own time.

2. Point out that, when someone decides to solve a problem or make a decision, he or she can use an *intuitive* approach, a *rational/analytical*

approach, or an approach that combines aspects of both. Distribute Training Instrument 11–19 as you display slide 9–16.

3. Provide a quick overview of the two approaches and then assign one of the two approaches to each small group. Show slide 9–17 and ask the groups to identify the strengths and weaknesses of the approach they have been assigned and to identify when to use and not use the approach. Ask groups to appoint a group leader and then give them five minutes to complete the exercise, making personal notes on the instrument as desired.

4. Reconvene the large group and facilitate the group reports. Record the groups' responses on flipchart paper if time permits. Some of the likely responses you may hear are presented in table 11–1.

5. When facilitating the discussion of the advantages and disadvantages of the intuitive approach, reinforce the group's responses as much as possible. Ask, *Where does our intuition come from?* Suggest that intuition—our gut instinct or response—comes from our past experience. Note that the more our past experience matches the current challenge or situation, the more useful our intuition is in solving the problem or making the decision. Suggest that the potential hazard of the intuitive approach is that we often are faced with new or unique challenges that may not match our experience base. In such instances, relying too much on intuition may not be the best practice. At the same time, for some unique situations our intuition may be the only thing we can fall back on when making the call.

6. Refer to the work of Gary Klein (*Sources of Power: How People Make Decisions,* 1998). Explain that Klein studied how people working in stressful, life-and-death situations (for example, firefighters, police officers, soldiers) solved problems and made decisions. Cite his findings that the sources of power people relied on were almost exclusively intuitive. Emphasize, however, that for these situations, repetitive training to drill experience into the intuitive subconscious was fundamental.

7. In facilitating the discussion of the rational/analytical approach to PSDM, note that this approach is the easier one to defend under scrutiny. Point out that because a rational/analytical decision is based on a careful analysis of the data, the decision is transparent.

Table 11–1

Sample Strengths, Weaknesses, and Occasions to Use PSDM Approaches

INTUITIVE APPROACH TO PSDM

Strengths

- Fast
- Based on history/experience
- Less influenced by group members without relevant experience

When to Use

- When you need quick action or a quick decision
- When you have past experience that is similar to the new situation
- When you don't have access to all of the relevant data
- When the right people with the right experience are using this approach

Weaknesses

- Past experience may not prepare the person for a new situation
- No documentation of the rationale used
- Marginalizes people with more limited experience

When NOT to Use

- When you or the decision makers don't have an experience base that is similar to the new situation
- If you need to document or justify how you solve the problem or make the decision
- When you need a broader consensus from those who may be asked to implement the actions or decision

RATIONAL/ANALYTICAL APPROACH TO PSDM

Strengths

- Defensible and transparent—the reasoning behind the actions or decisions is clear
- Based on real data, not hunches
- Provides an opportunity for participation

When to Use

- When you need to be able to defend your PSDM process
- When you have the data
- When you have the time
- When you need an inclusive process

Weaknesses

- Can be very slow
- Analysis paralysis may set in—too much analysis isn't always the best way to proceed
- Is only as good as the data you have
- Without relevant data, it's hard to use this approach

When NOT to Use

- When time is critical
- When you don't have access to relevant data
- When the decision has already been made (using another approach)

One of the clear benefits of this approach, then, is that you are able to show in detail how you came to your solution or decision.

8. Contrast the two approaches by noting that one challenge of the intuitive approach is its lack of transparency: The method you used to solve the problem or make the decision is not always obvious or defensible. Sometimes saying "my gut told me to do this" doesn't cut it when arguing your case before the board of directors, your manager, or other departments.

DEBRIEFING

◆ Reiterate that both approaches are legitimate means for solving problems and making decisions. The key is when to use each of them—or both of them together.

◆ Stress that strategic PSDM involves knowing when to base our short- and long-term actions and decisions on our "gut" instincts or on a careful and thoughtful analysis of the environment.

◆ Point out that some of the great corporate success stories were not the result of fancy analysis—just the intuitive hunch by the CEO or other key leaders that going in a certain direction was the absolutely right thing to do.

Learning Activity 11–23: Applying the Strategic Problem-Solving Model

OBJECTIVES

The objectives of this learning activity are to

◆ introduce a model to guide strategic problem solving

◆ enable participants to apply the model to a specific issue in the organization.

MATERIALS

◆ PowerPoint slides 9–18 through 9–20

◆ Handout 11–23: A Model for Problem Solving

◆ Flipchart, easel, and marker for each small group

TIME

◆ 65 minutes

PREPARATION

◆ Select or identify a specific organizational problem to solve during the activity. Choose the problem by tapping into issues that participants identified earlier in the day, by talking with managers or leaders prior to the workshop, or by drawing from your own experience with the organization. The problem you choose, however, should be one about which most participants will have some prior knowledge or perspective. For the greatest benefit, select a problem that is seen as relevant and important to the group you're working with.

◆ State the problem on a flipchart page or on a PowerPoint slide. (Have either or both of these problem statements ready for use during the activity, but don't post them before the appropriate time.) Keep the problem statement somewhat vague or general in nature. One of the key lessons for participants here is the importance of defining the problem. The value of keeping your description of the problem vague is that it requires participants to define it more specifically.

INSTRUCTIONS

1. Introduce the formal step-by-step problem-solving model by distributing Handout 11–23. Acknowledge that this model springs from the rational/analytical approach to problem solving—but that it provides ample opportunity for the intuitive approach to assert itself when necessary. Note that this rational/analytical model is presented in part because most organizations require transparent problem-solving approaches that reveal the underlying thinking. Indicate that this is especially important when attempting to enlist commitment from others to the solution chosen. Point out, however, that there are times (as discussed in Learning Activity 11–22) when the pure rational/analytical approach is *not* the one to use.

2. Walk the large group quickly through the step-by-step model by displaying slide 9–18. Take questions from the group as you go. Emphasize key points along the way so that participants understand the key outcomes from each step of the process.

Make a special point of emphasizing the importance of spending time exploring the *causes* of the problem. Encourage the group to avoid the alluring trap of defining the problem and then jumping right to solutions. Ask them to slow down, rather than speed up, in their approach to problem solving. State that "going slower will get you to the solution faster!"

3. Indicate that you'd like them to use the model to solve a real problem facing the organization. Reveal the problem statement you prepared before the workshop, and ask each group to locate its flipchart and marker. Ask groups to select a group leader and a member who will record their work on the flipchart. Emphasize that the groups *must* use their flipcharts as a way of focusing their energy; keeping track of their definitions, findings, and insights; and communicating their work to others in the room.

4. Instruct groups to begin working through the first five steps of the model. Emphasize that, given the short amount of time they will have—30 minutes—they should focus most of their energy on the first *three* steps. Tell them to skip step 4 if they find themselves running out of time. Explain that when you call time, you'll expect each group to report its recommended actions.

5. Walk around the room to monitor the group activities. Give assistance, direction, and support where necessary. Don't pull groups back from making mistakes or going in the wrong direction. Let the process unfold in its own way. About 15 minutes into the work, indicate that they have just 15 minutes left and that they should manage their time carefully.

6. Regardless of where groups are in the problem-solving process, reconvene the large group when 30 minutes have passed. Ask for any general reactions to the step-by-step model. Did they find it difficult? Easy? Did they have enough time?

7. Ask group leaders to share findings and recommendations. Bring all groups' results to the whole class. Ask participants to compare and contrast the results they achieved with results from other groups.

8. Give particular attention to how each group defined the problem. Point out variations among groups. Ask what might cause the groups to define the problem differently? Acknowledge that you intention-

ally gave them an *ambiguous* problem statement to see how they would clarify and focus the problem. Explore if these different problem statements led to different causes and different solutions.

9. Display slide 9–19 as you ask the large group of participants to identify what factors influenced or shaped how they worked through the problem-solving process and how they got their results.

10. Display slide 9–20. It highlights some of the common factors that influence the problem-solving process. Note that, although time was a major issue in their deliberations, many of the same issues and challenges that they experienced would also be experienced by any problem-solving team working in any timeframe.

DEBRIEFING

- ◆ Emphasize that defining the problem statement early and clearly is fundamental to successful problem solving. Note that varying solutions that groups chose to address the problem may have sprung, in part, from their different definitions of the problem.

- ◆ Stress that differences in strategy don't mean someone is right and someone is wrong—it just means they may have solved different problems!

- ◆ Highlight, as well, the importance of exploring *cause* before moving toward solutions. Emphasize that individuals and groups too often leap directly from defining a problem to exploring solutions. They skip the key step of identifying forces and factors that caused the problem and likely are sustaining it. Without understanding and addressing the causes of a problem, we are likely to see the problem return.

- ◆ Note that the problem-solving model that the groups explored in this learning activity is drawn largely from the rational/analytical approach. Acknowledge that sometimes this is the perfect model to use and sometimes it would be a very poor choice.

Learning Activity 11–24: What Is Your Imagination Quotient?

OBJECTIVES

The objectives of this learning activity are to

- introduce a fun activity to change the tempo and energy in the room

- develop participant awareness of the importance of divergent thinking to PSDM.

MATERIALS

- PowerPoint slides 9–21 through 9–25

- Training Instrument 11–20: Your Imagination Quotient

- Prize for the winning team, if desired

TIME

- 30 minutes

PREPARATION

- Complete one copy of Training Instrument 11–20 with the "answers" (located at the end of this activity) so you can provide the answers just in case participants don't discover them.

INSTRUCTIONS

1. Distribute Training Instrument 11–20 and display slide 11–21. Ask small groups to work as teams to see how quickly they can answer each of the IQ puzzles. Give groups about eight minutes to complete the quiz.

2. If you wish, you can promise some sort of prize for the group that gets them all right. **Note:** We recommend something that the winning team can share with others in the class—a bag of candy, for example.

3. Reconvene the full group and walk participants through the puzzles. Show the appropriate slides (11–22 through 11–25) to answer the graphic puzzles.

4. At the end of the activity, ask if any group got all of them correct. Distribute the prize or prizes, if desired.

5. Ask the large group why you had them complete the Imagination Quotient quiz. Reinforce what some participants will likely say: solving many of the puzzles required them to change their ways of looking at something. They required out-of-the-box thinking, which is exactly what strategic problem solving requires—bringing a fresh perspective to long-lasting challenges. Remind them of the seven guiding principles of PSDM, noting the importance of viewing each problem for its uniqueness and from a fresh perspective—through the "eyes of a child."

DEBRIEFING

◆ Remind participants that strategic PSDM requires a splash of creativity and imagination to escape solving the same problem in the same way—over and over again. Encourage them to strengthen their imagination quotient as they approach the real challenges they face in the organization.

ANSWERS TO THE IQ QUIZ

1. The beetle can be inside or outside the box. The trick is that one of the side corner lines of the box crosses the beetle at its midsection.

2. Sandbox

3. Man overboard

4. I understand

5. Both an elegant woman *and* an elderly woman.

6. Tricycle

7. Downtown

8. Neon light (official). "Light Bologna" (unofficial) is also allowed—*very* divergent thinking!

9. Life after death

10. Three degrees below zero

11. The ambiguous "shadows" suggest a variety of personas to people over time: Many participants cite Jesus; some suggest Che Guevara; more recently, participants have identified Osama bin Laden.

12. Circles under the eyes

13. Backward glance

14. He's beside himself

15. Scrambled eggs

16. Split level

17. Touchdown

18. Paradise

19. Reading between the lines

20. Six feet underground

21. See slide 9–25 for the most common method—but there are more unconventional solutions to this challenge.

Learning Activity 11–25: Writing the Problem Statement

Because this activity typically follows Learning Activity 11–23 (Applying the Strategic Problem-Solving Model) in sequence within your workshop, it will help participants address the first challenge of any problem-solving process: clearly defining the problem.

OBJECTIVES

The objectives of this learning activity are to

♦ identify the characteristics of a good problem statement

♦ apply the characteristics to sample problem statements with the goal of improving their clarity.

MATERIALS

♦ PowerPoint slides 9–26 through 9–29

♦ Handout 11–24: Writing Clear Problem Statements

♦ Training Instrument 11–21: What's the Problem?

TIME

♦ 45 minutes

PREPARATION

♦ You may want to customize Training Instrument 11–21 to reflect some of the problems that participants identified either prior to or at the start of the workshop. Because the goal of the exercise is to improve participant skills in writing a problem statement, the sample problems you present to the group should be general, abstract, or even confusing! If you have customized Training Instrument 11–21, make sure that you develop a "good" problem statement for every "bad" one and that you share them with the group at the end of the activity.

INSTRUCTIONS

1. Display slide 9–26. Note that the quote from Malcolm Forbes, a very successful U.S. business leader, points out one of the major challenges of problem solving: understanding the problem. Suggest that a clear understanding begins with a clear and precise definition of the problem.

2. Note that, in your own experience, 90 percent of solving a problem is being clear on (and where the solving involves more than one person, agreeing about) the definition of the problem statement. Call attention to the results from Learning Activity 11–23 (if you have conducted this activity with the group), pointing out that how individual groups framed the problem determined the path that they recommended for solving the problem.

3. Begin displaying slide 9–27 as you distribute Handout 11–24. Talk participants through the key characteristics of a good problem statement, as presented on the slide and the handout. As you finish this list, note that writing a problem statement is more art than science—but that groups need to do a much better job of thinking through exactly what the problem is before they rush to solve it.

4. Invite and answer any questions from the group before distributing Training Instrument 11–21 and showing slide 9–28. Introduce the small-group portion of this activity by noting that this instrument has six problem statements in the left-hand column and that over the next 10 minutes the groups will write six clearer problem statements, drawing from Handout 11–24 for insights into how to write a good statement.

5. Depending on the number of people in the workshop and therefore the number of small groups, assign each group one or two of the statements. Ask each group to select a group leader who will guide the discussion and report findings.

6. About halfway through the exercise, announce the time remaining.

7. Reconvene the large group and facilitate a discussion of each of the problem statements. Ask each group leader to offer the group's improved statement(s), and reinforce any of the positive aspects of their recommended statements as you offer your own.

   Note: If you use Training Instrument 11–21 as is, display slides 9–28 and 9–29, which present our recommended statements. Be sure to indicate that, in many cases, drafting an improved statement involves just deciding the direction you will take the problem. Explain that "narrowing" the problem means that you focus on one aspect of a larger issue. Doing this may be exactly what's required—or it may be ducking the real issue. Each person or problem-solving group must declare a clear focus, communicate this focus to itself and others as required, and then move into subsequent stages of solution seeking.

DEBRIEFING

   ◆ Note that the quality of every problem-solving process is profoundly shaped by the quality of the problem definition. Getting it right at the start of the process significantly improves one's chances of finding a lasting solution.

   ◆ Acknowledge that crafting clear problem statements is difficult work. It *shouldn't* be easy—and if it is, we've probably not looked deeply enough into the problem.

Learning Activity 11–26: Applying the Strategic Decision-Making Model

OBJECTIVES

The objectives of this learning activity are to

   ◆ introduce a model for strategic decision making

   ◆ enable participants to apply the strategic decision-making model to a specific example.

MATERIALS

- ◆ PowerPoint slides 9–30 and 9–31

- ◆ Handout 11–25: A Model for Strategic Decision Making

- ◆ Handout 11–26: The Decision Matrix

- ◆ Training Instrument 11–22: Applying the Decision Matrix

- ◆ Paper and pencils at each table

- ◆ Flipchart, easel, and marker for each group

TIME

- ◆ 60 minutes

PREPARATION

- ◆ If you decide to customize Training Instrument 11–22 and use a decision-making example drawn from participants (or from leaders and managers or your own experience with the organization), make adjustments to the instrument before the workshop.

INSTRUCTIONS

1. Explain that in this activity participants will learn a model for making decisions when faced with a choice of options.

2. Note that much of this model, like the model for problem solving, is grounded in the rational/analytical approach to problem solving (refer to Learning Activity 11–22 if necessary). It presumes that you need to use more than an intuitive hunch when making your decision—or that you need to justify or defend the decision you finally make.

3. Distribute Handout 11–25 as you display slide 9–30. Ask participants to read through the step-by-step decision-making model on their own and to jot down any questions they have or anything that is not clear.

4. If participants have completed Learning Activity 11–23 (Applying the Strategic Problem-Solving Model), ask them to note the differences between that model for problem solving and this one. Give individuals a couple of minutes to read the handout.

5. Invite and answer any questions about the decision-making model. If contrasting the model with the problem-solving model, ask what are the main differences between the models (for example, there is no exploration of *cause* for the decision-making model, the decision-making model requires a clarification of our *requirements,* alternatives or choices need to be defined).

6. Call the group's attention back to the decision-making model, highlighting the importance of step 2 of the process: *Define your desired objectives/outcomes/purpose.* Stress the importance of this step in making a good decision, and ask why this step is so critical to the process. At least one participant should make the point that the choice one finally makes (from among alternatives) *must be based* on the underlying needs that you want to satisfy with the decision. Suggest that like the issue of *cause* for problem solving, defining your *musts* and *wants* is central to making the right decision.

7. As you distribute Handout 11–26, say that you're giving them an essential tool for sorting out the *musts* and *wants* in a given situation and for applying them to the decision choices. Ask them to take the next several minutes to read the material describing how the matrix works. Encourage them to note anything that is not clear or any questions they have.

8. After a couple of minutes, reconvene the large group and ask for any questions or needed clarifications to the process. When you have addressed all the issues raised, explain that they will next have an opportunity to apply the matrix in making a decision.

9. Distribute Training Instrument 11–22 (or a customized version of it that reflects a decision example specific to your organization) and display the decision matrix on slide 9–31. Point out the focus of the decision and the decision options or choices that they will be comparing.

10. Acknowledge that, although this example and the choices are somewhat abbreviated for simplicity's sake in this workshop, the example will give them a chance to practice applying the *musts* and *wants* to a specific decision.

11. Step through the components of the sample decision matrix by clicking through the explanation text on slide 9–31.

12. Ask participants to reform their small groups and select group leaders. Encourage them to use their flipcharts for developing the matrix and as a way to record their *musts/wants*. Give the groups 15 to 20 minutes for this activity.

13. About halfway through the allotted time, remind participants of the remaining time.

14. Reconvene the large group and ask each leader to identify the choice his or her group recommends.

15. Facilitate a discussion of both the results and the process the groups used. Ask such questions as these:

    a. Did all of the groups reach the same choice? Why or why not?

    b. What were their reactions to applying the decision matrix? Did they like the method? Did they find it too focused on numbers?

    c. When and if the total points of two options were the same or close, how did they handle the decision?

    d. Should a group always go with the highest-scoring option? When might doing this cause a problem? When wouldn't a group go exclusively with the numbers?

    e. What if, after the numbers are in, you feel uncomfortable with the winner? What might this suggest and what would you do? **Note:** Discomfort with a winning choice may suggest that there is another *must/want* that is not in the matrix. This situation generally requires clarifying this new *must/want* and then applying it again to all of the options. Be careful here, however, because this just may be a sneaky way to get the choice that one may have been leaning toward all along!

16. Point out that the decision-making model and the decision matrix require that participants in the process have access to information on their underlying needs (*musts/wants*) and on the choices before them (the degree to which each choice satisfies the *must/want*). Without good data—real data—the matrix can easily fall apart. Although this doesn't mean you can't make the decision (you may end up with an *intuitive* decision), it does make it harder to reach agreement or to justify the final choice you have made.

DEBRIEFING

◆ Reiterate that the decision-making model and the decision matrix tool are powerful techniques to help an individual or group identify what the solution really needs to address.

◆ As an example, cite this year's family vacation. Before one starts booking flights or reserving cabins, the family needs to discuss and agree on the *must/want* criteria. Without agreement on these—or without at least a healthy discussion—the final choice the family makes will be frustrating to some, if not all, family members.

◆ Point out that the decision-making model and matrix can buffer the bias or influence of individuals in the group. Forcing the decision-making team to identify its *musts/wants* and then evaluate how "good" each choice is at satisfying those *musts/wants* makes the decision more rational/analytical and less influenced by individual players.

Learning Activity 11–27: Involving Others in Strategic PSDM

OBJECTIVES

The objectives of this learning activity are to

◆ reveal the benefits and advantages of involving others in strategic PSDM

◆ identify some considerations for when one should or should not involve others in strategic PSDM.

MATERIALS

◆ PowerPoint slides 9–32 and 9–33

◆ Handout 11–27: When to Involve or Not Involve Others

◆ Training Instrument 11–23: When Is It Time to Involve Others?

◆ Flipchart page and marker

TIME

◆ 25 minutes

PREPARATION

◆ Prepare a flipchart page divided in half vertically. The left half of the page should be titled *When to Involve Others* and the right half should be titled *When NOT to Involve Others.*

INSTRUCTIONS

1. Note that there is a lot of emphasis on participation and involvement in PSDM. Suggest that this is a good thing—but that participation and involvement are not always helpful or appropriate. Distribute Training Instrument 11–23 and display slide 9–32. Ask small groups to take the next five minutes to identify when it is appropriate, good, and even essential to involve others and when it may be less desirable or appropriate. Ask them to write their group's thoughts in the left and right columns of Training Instrument 11–23.

2. Reconvene the full group and invite participants to say when it is appropriate and desirable to involve others. Write these in the left-hand column of the prepared flipchart page.

3. When the left-hand column is filled in, gather ideas from the group and record them in the right-hand column of the page.

4. Summarize the ideas offered by the group and then distribute Handout 11–27, guidelines for involving/not involving others. Highlight how important it is for any PSDM team to consider these factors when weighing the issue of inclusion.

5. Draw participants' attention to the note at the end of the *Involvement Is Unnecessary . . .* column. Explain that although the reasons listed for *not involving* others are sound, often it may be important to *work with* others to negotiate their disagreements, educate and enlighten them, manage group dynamics more effectively, develop their knowledge base, and so forth. Suggest that involving others in a decision (especially when the consequences of being wrong are not significant) can develop the wisdom and competence of the group and enhance its *future* PSDM. Point out that an effective problem solver/decision maker will look at each PSDM situation and make an informed judgment regarding whether to involve others and the best approach for doing so.

6. Display slide 9–33, showing the continuum of decision-making options—from autocratic (*I decide*), to democratic (*we decide*), to empowered (*you decide*). Emphasize that each approach is appropriate in its own way, and that each has potentially good and bad consequences when used. Point out that strategic problem solvers and decision makers simply need to pause and consider the level and degree of involvement that is most appropriate for their situation.

7. Make the case that participation simply for its own sake is just "feel-good" management—but participation for the sake of improving the way in which a problem is solved or a decision is made makes a difference in the quality of the end result.

DEBRIEFING

Display slide 9–34 to emphasize that participation and involvement are important for two primary reasons: (1) they increase the likelihood of defining the problem/decision correctly and understanding the context of the problem/decision—including the underlying causes and identifying critical *musts/wants*; and (2) they can powerfully and positively influence the level of commitment to the decision or solution in those who are asked to implement it.

Learning Activity 11–28: Introducing the Strategic PSDM Tool Kit and Prioritizing the Tools

OBJECTIVES

The objectives of this learning activity are to

- introduce the variety of tools contained in the Strategic PSDM Tool Kit
- identify when each tool can be used within the strategic PSDM process
- introduce a simple method any group can use to quickly prioritize a list of choices.

MATERIALS

- PowerPoint slides 10–7 and 10–8
- Handout 11–28: Strategic PSDM Tool Kit

♦ Red and blue sticky-dots (half-inch circles are ideal), one red and four blue dots for each person

♦ Flipchart page and marker

TIME

♦ 30 minutes

PREPARATION

♦ Place one red and four blue sticky-dots at each place on the tables.

♦ Prepare a flipchart page that lists each tool in the Tool Kit on its own line and draw horizontal lines to separate the individual tools. Leave space in front of the name of each tool for people to place sticky-dot "votes." See figure 11–4 for an idea of what this flipchart page might look like. **Note:** If this workshop follows the one-day Strategic Problem Solving and Decision Making workshop and participants had the opportunity to practice the Decision Matrix tool (excerpted from the Tool Kit), you may decide to exclude this tool from the list on the flipchart page.

INSTRUCTIONS

1. Distribute Handout 11–28 as you display slide 10–7. Introduce the activity by noting that this tool kit contains some of the most useful PSDM tools available.

2. Call attention to the kit's contents and review the structure of the Tool Kit. Note that the PSDM models are on pages TK-2 and TK-3.

3. Ask participants to turn to the Strategic Problem-Solving Model. Call attention to the seven steps of the problem-solving model and note that each tool in the Tool Kit is listed—in some cases, several times—in the right-hand column of the model. Note that, depending on which stage of the problem-solving process they are engaged in, there are various tools to help teams with that stage. Note that the strategic decision-making model is displayed next and the tools are again matched to each stage of the process.

4. Indicate to the group that, for the balance of today's workshop, their focus exclusively will be on practicing and applying most of these

Figure 11–4

Sample Flipchart Page for Sticky-Dot Voting

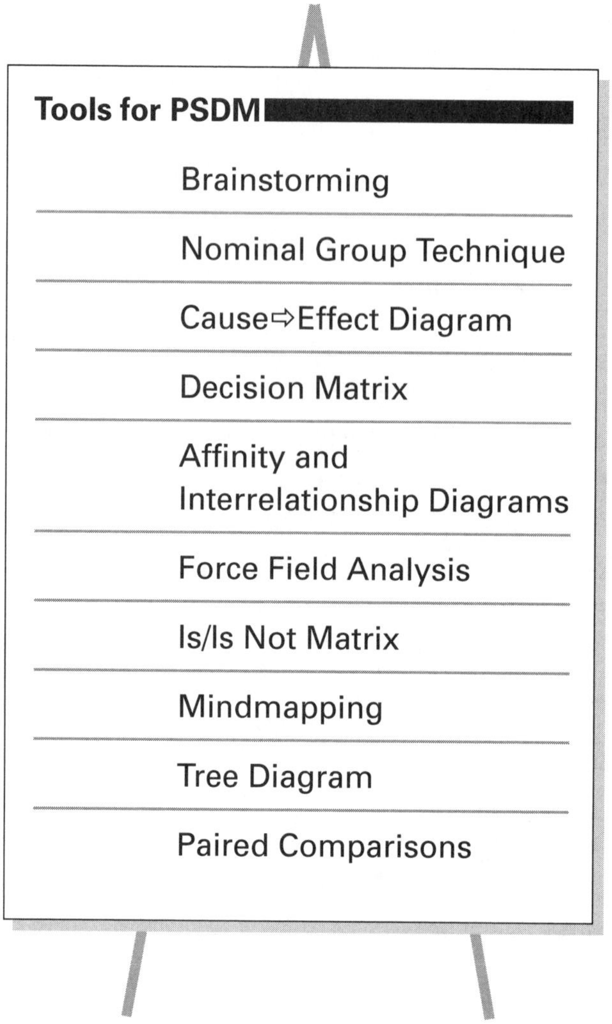

Tools for PSDM

Brainstorming

Nominal Group Technique

Cause⇨Effect Diagram

Decision Matrix

Affinity and
Interrelationship Diagrams

Force Field Analysis

Is/Is Not Matrix

Mindmapping

Tree Diagram

Paired Comparisons

tools. Acknowledge that time constraints may make it impossible to get to each tool so you would like them to begin by prioritizing the list of tools, rank-ordering them from most important to practice to least important to practice.

5. Call attention to the sticky-dots at their places. Point out that they'll use these dots to decide which tools you'll focus on for the balance of the day.

6. Point out the prepared flipchart page on which you've listed all of the tools. **Note:** If you decided to exclude the Decision Matrix from

this list (see note in Preparations above), point out that this tool is not listed because the group already worked with it.

7. Display slide 10–8. Explain that over the next 10 minutes they will be reading through the Tool Kit and casting their votes (sticky-dots) for the five tools they would most want to practice today. Tell them to use the red sticky-dot to designate the most important tool to practice and to use the blue dots to identify their four second-priority tools to practice during the workshop.

8. Explain how the voting process will work: They will read through the Tool Kit and then take their red and blue dots to the posted flipchart page that lists the tools. They'll place their dots beside their first- and second-priority tools. Ask if participants have any questions about the voting process. Remind them that this is a solo activity, and that when they have finished reviewing the tools, they should cast their votes for the five tools that they want to practice.

9. Draw participants' attention to the Brainstorming page of the Tool Kit. Indicate that this page is structured like all other Tool Kit pages: There is an introduction that generally describes the use and function of the specific tool, followed by the steps necessary to use the tool.

10. Tell them that you would like them to take the next 10 minutes to read just these introductory paragraphs for all of the tools. **Note:** If you decided to exclude the Decision Matrix, point out this fact and tell them to skip that tool's description.

11. Tell them to begin voting when they've read the explanations of the tools.

12. As participants begin placing their sticky-dots on the flipchart, track the distribution of dots and begin planning your next steps. As a trend begins to form in the distribution of dots (for example, as you see reds clustering or a preponderance of dots being placed beside one or another tool), arrange your slides and, if appropriate, flipchart pages to reflect the group's likely priorities.

13. As the last participant to vote is placing his or her dots, begin tallying the votes. The red dots count for two points and the blues count for one. Develop a total score for each tool. Write and circle this total beside each tool. **Note:** You can ask one of the participants to de-

velop this tally while you guide a discussion of the sticky-dot voting method. If you decide to request a participant's help for this, elicit his or her help early in the voting process.

14. Before calling attention to the final tally, elicit reactions from the group to the sticky-dot technique. Ask, *What did you think of this way of voting? Did the process/method work for you? What did you like or not like about the sticky-dot approach for determining a group's priorities?*

15. Draw participants into a discussion of the merits and disadvantages of this method. Summarize the discussion of the technique by making the following points:

    a. As with any PSDM tool, there are advantages and disadvantages to the tool and it's important to recognize them so we can make an informed choice about using a tool.

    b. Note the advantages of the sticky-dot voting technique: It's fun; it's a fast way to rank-order a list of issues; it eliminates discussion, debate, and argument; it offers a very quick feel for the sentiments of the group as the colors and trends appear; and it can get an indecisive group unstuck and free it to begin discussing its priorities.

    c. There are potential disadvantages to this type of voting: People can be influenced by the votes already recorded; the first and last voters have the most influence over the outcome either by setting a trend or by making the decision to break a tie between two issues with the same number of votes; the process is public so there is no anonymity; and participants can stuff the ballot box by placing all of their votes on one choice.

    d. In many situations the advantages will outweigh the disadvantages, but in other circumstances a different technique (such as the nominal group technique outlined in the Tool Kit) might be preferred. Remind participants that every technique carries its own advantages and disadvantages and that they should consider these when deciding which method to use within the PSDM process.

16. Point out that the sticky-dot voting technique is not in the Tool Kit—it's a bonus tool that they can easily use throughout the PSDM process for choosing which problem to focus on, for identifying which causes are most important, and for deciding which solution is best.

17. Indicate that, as time permits, you will try to organize the workshop to give the group time to practice *all* of the tools—but that you will work through their priority list to ensure that the tools they identified as most important are practiced first.

DEBRIEFING

◆ Note that the PSDM Tool Kit will be the focus of the balance of today's workshop, beginning with tools the group identified as most important to practice and apply.

◆ Remind participants that the Tool Kit, while offering the more useful and accessible tools, does not exhaust the array of tools that one can use in the PSDM process. Note that there are many other tools they can draw from when solving problems and making decisions and that they are encouraged to explore additional tools when they have mastered these. Cite additional references for their use beyond the workshop.

Learning Activity 11–29: Applying the Strategic PSDM Tools

Because the focus of this activity is entirely determined by the voting process in Learning Activity 11–28, keep the design of this learning activity flexible.

OBJECTIVES

The objectives of this learning activity are to

◆ practice the highest-priority tools contained in the Strategic PSDM Tool Kit using, to the greatest extent possible, the real issues, challenges, and problems identified by the organization's leadership or the participants

◆ discuss the advantages and disadvantages of each tool practiced.

MATERIALS

◆ PowerPoint slides 10–9 through 10–16, used according to the priorities determined by participants

◆ Handout 11–28: Strategic PSDM Tool Kit

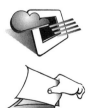

- Additional handouts and training instruments from this book as desired (particularly Training Instrument 11–22 for assistance with the Decision Matrix)

- Flipchart, easel, and marker for each table and at least two for facilitator use at the front of the room

- Sticky-notes and fine-point, felt-tip pens at each place

TIME

- 3 hours, 35 minutes

PREPARATION

- If possible, prepare flipchart pages or PowerPoint slides for all of the PSDM tools, based on ideas from the organization's leaders or participants. Ideally, these flipchart pages or slides would be prepared in anticipation that groups will identify certain issues and certain tools as high-priority items. If you prepare to use all of the tools and identify specific issues/topics for each of them, you will be ready for whatever direction participants decide to go.

- Decide how you will teach each tool and what issues you will address with each tool.

- Consider team-teaching this learning activity. Doing so can significantly reduce the pressure on you as you customize the workshop *on the hoof.* For example, while you are leading the group through applying one of the tools, your teaching partner can be preparing to lead the group through the next chosen tool.

INSTRUCTIONS

1. Start with the PSDM tool that received the most points in sticky-dot voting. Here's the process you should follow for each tool:

    a. Identify the tool to practice and the number of the page where it appears in the Tool Kit. Ask everyone to turn to that page.

    b. Have available a slide or flipchart page that describes the tool. (Create these from the descriptive paragraphs at the beginning of each tool in the Tool Kit.)

c. Shift participants' attention to the front of the room where you have a flipchart page, slide, whiteboard, or wallchart that you will use to demonstrate the use of the tool.

d. Briefly demonstrate an application of the tool and then direct participants to work in their small groups to practice the tool.

e. For some of the tools (especially the affinity diagram, the nominal group process, and mindmapping) lead the group as a whole through the tool demonstration. There may or may not be small-group activities when you are leading a large-group tool demonstration.

f. Before turning the groups loose on applying the tool, provide very clear instructions on using the tool and on their assigned task. Generally you will give all of the groups the same issue, challenge, problem, and so forth. This will facilitate a useful discussion of the results of each tool and of how different groups may or may not have achieved different results.

g. Give groups a specific timeframe for completing their application of the tool and being prepared to report their responses. Encourage groups to assign a timekeeper to keep them on track—but indicate that you will also be providing timechecks to help them stay on schedule.

h. Instruct the groups to use the flipcharts and other equipment available to them.

2. In line with the preliminary planning you did for addressing each tool, present the tools according to the priority ranking that participants chose:

   ◆ **Brainstorming:** Highlight the two approaches to brainstorming (structured and unstructured). This tool may best be demonstrated by you leading the entire group through the two approaches. You may want to divide the group in two and use the *structured* process for one half and the *unstructured* for the other half. Use the same topic for both approaches, but don't reveal this until it is evident in the exercise itself. Highlight the principles for brainstorming (summarized on slide 10–9) before practicing the tool. Begin with the *structured* approach, revealing the flipchart page and asking those in the structured activity to write down their ideas. After you have guided the reporting of 15 to 20 of the ideas from this group, stop the activity and move to the *un-structured* approach. Reveal the flipchart page that indicates the same topic and lead that process, working as quickly as possible to record the ideas from those people involved in this approach. Debrief by asking the groups which approach each prefers and why and when it would or would not use each approach.

◆ **Nominal Group Technique:** Structure this activity to follow the brainstorming activity if both are in the priority list of tools. Save time by noting that the first four steps of this technique are what was done in the *structured* brainstorming activity. If, however, this technique is being covered alone, demonstrate the activity by selecting half of the class and leading them step-by-step through the process. Because the full process in the real world can take as much as two hours, acknowledge that you will abbreviate the process—but make sure you demonstrate and explain each of its steps, even if you shorten the reporting or clarification times. Debrief by asking when such a tool would be most helpful (for example, when wanting to reduce the effects of group interaction, when there is a history of contention and disagreement in the group) and when it would be less helpful.

◆ **Cause ⇨ Effect Diagram:** Demonstrate the power of this tool by using the "Dead Zone" in the Gulf of Mexico. Explain that in the Gulf there is an area greater than 5,800 square miles (as of 2004—the amount varies from year to year) that is completely devoid of marine life. Ask participants if they can guess where the dead zone is located in the Gulf. Note that the dead zone begins where the Mississippi River empties into the Gulf of Mexico. Tell participants that the dead zone is the effect of a host of causes. Ask them this question: *If you were a marine biologist, where would you go to find the causes of the dead zone?* Agree with the responses, noting that you would have to go up river to identify the origins of the problem.

Display slide 10–10 and point out that the Mississippi River is the main channel leading to the "effect" and that each of the "branches" (ribs in the "fish bone" diagram—another term for the diagram) represents a different river: the Ohio, the Missouri, the Illinois, the Wisconsin, and so forth. Click through the text on this slide, noting that each river or branch makes its own contributions to the mix in the Mississippi River, leading to the final result in the Gulf dead zone. **Note:** When revealing and discussing the assigned causes for each river, point out that these examples are your guesses and likely represent only a few of the potential pollutants in any of these rivers.

Then explain that in the workplace, each of the branches is commonly labeled as displayed in slide 10–11. Present the specific workplace issue or topic to be explored and ask the groups to develop their own cause⇨effect diagrams on their flipcharts (they may want to tear off a page and place it on the table in a landscape format). Debrief reactions to the tool.

◆ **Decision Matrix:** Given the complexity of this tool, it will be difficult to guide the group through one of the issues that they identified earlier in the day. Because the Decision Matrix requires considerable pre-work (identifying the decision and the decision choices/options, identifying the decision requirements, and gathering data on how well each decision choice meets each decision requirement), we recommend that you have a clear plan for this tool and that you prepare your materials long in advance of the workshop. We suggest you pursue one of the following two teaching options:

a. *Decision Matrix Option 1:* If the tool hasn't already been taught to the group in a strategic PSDM workshop, distribute Training Instrument 11–22 (from Learning Activity 11–26) and ask participants to focus on this instrument rather than on Handout 11–28. Display slide 10–12 to demonstrate how the process works and then ask the groups to follow the additional steps of the process as outlined in Training Instrument 11–22. Debrief by asking the groups to share their decisions and the numbers behind their decisions. As time permits, explore some of the reflection questions suggested in Training Instrument 11–22. If you wish, display slide 10–13 to demonstrate one possible outcome of the exercise. Note, however, that this is only an example of how the process works and is not necessarily the "correct" decision. End the application of this tool by highlighting its rational/ analytical focus and noting that it is important to capture critical data on the *musts/wants* and the characteristics of each choice or option.

b. ***Decision Matrix Option 2:*** If you use one of the decision issues identified by the organization's leadership in advance of the workshop, prepare workshop materials (using the Decision Matrix template in Handout 11–28) that define the decision to be made, the choices/options, and the decision requirements. Then share this partially filled-in matrix with the group and ask them to complete it. You may want to modify Learning Activity 11–26 and Training Instrument 11–22 to reflect the organization-specific example.

◆ **Affinity and Interrelationship Diagrams:** Given the complexity of this tool, we recommend that you lead the entire group through the full process. Select the topic to focus on and direct participants to use the supplied sticky-notes and fine-point marking pens to respond to the issue you have posted on a flipchart or on a slide. When it is time for placing and organizing the sticky-notes, direct groups to use their flipcharts. Have teams report their groupings and category titles. For the interrelationship diagramming portion of the tool, select one group's flipchart page and lead the large group in identifying the causation relationships. Depending on the time you have available, direct all of the groups to work independently to finish diagramming the relationships between the categories identified by the sample group. Complete the tool by discussing the I/O relationships and the importance of identifying the primary drivers/influencers. Debrief participant reactions to the tool and ask them to describe when the tool would be especially useful (for example, when dealing with large and ambiguous topics that you want to better understand).

◆ **Force Field Analysis:** Demonstrate the force field analysis tool by applying the tool to a personal situation (for example, wishing one had a body like an Olympic champion!) and the forces that are driving you to accomplish this and those that are restraining (preventing) you from achieving this. Invite the large group to help you identify these driving and restraining forces—have some fun with this. Slide 10–14 offers one take on this example. Identify the issue that you want the groups to work on and then direct participants to complete the force field analysis (using their flipcharts). Debrief by exploring the usefulness of this tool (in helping them understand the broad array of forces that influence movement on an issue) and its limitations (for example, it doesn't tell users *how* to reduce the restraining forces and strengthen the driving forces).

◆ **Is/Is Not Matrix:** Walk the group through the example provided in the Tool Kit and displayed on slide 10–15. Then identify a specific problem for the tool and direct small groups to fill in a matrix for the problem on their flipcharts. Debrief by noting that this is a powerful tool for narrowing and focusing a problem statement. It reminds us what actually is working so we can focus on what is *not* working. It also allows us to understand the influence of a problem—and, as a result, to grasp how urgent it is that we do something about the problem.

◆ **Mindmapping:** This activity is best led by you at a prepared wallchart or whiteboard. Select a topic to focus on and invite participants to gather around the wallchart or whiteboard. Follow the steps described in the Tool Kit. As time permits, present another topic for the groups to work on at their own flipcharts. Debrief by making the point that this is a powerful tool for understanding all of the forces influencing the "center" of the map. For those who participated in the half-day workshop on developing strategic thinkers, note the similarities with the Strategic Issues Map that was developed in that workshop.

◆ **Tree Diagram:** Display slide 10–16 that portrays a tree diagram. Click through the highlights on this slide, noting the emerging details as one moves to the right of the diagram. Indicate that the "leaves" provide the greatest detail—and that some level of detail would need to be developed for each one of the "limbs" to complete the diagramming process.

Ask for and answer questions about the diagramming process. Shift to the development of a tree diagram for the issue you have chosen for the group (chosen from among their own issues). Name the goal or desired outcome. Guide small groups through the process step by step. Ask each group to develop the major branches (subgoals) first. After they have identified the main branches for accomplishing the goal, direct them to select ONE of the major branches and to develop the "limbs" under it. Encourage them to use a new flipchart page if desired. Point out that using sticky-notes can help them sort out the sequence of activities. Have the groups report their branch subgoals and, as time permits, have one or two groups report their "limbs." Because of the level of detail typically required for defining the "twigs/leaves," note that the groups won't be moving to this level of the tree diagram during the workshop. Debrief participants' reactions to the tree diagramming process.

♦ **Paired Comparison:** Note the value of this tool in helping a group rank-order a list of choices or options by applying selection criteria. Given the amount of development work required for this activity, it's best that you lead this from the front of the room, using an example that you have prepared in advance.

Have each of the ideas or choices you have identified (from step 1 of the process) on a separate sticky-note, arranged in a single column (in no particular order) on a flipchart page or whiteboard. On the same page or whiteboard, write the simple criteria for evaluating the "goodness" of the choices (try to limit yourself to no more than three criteria). Tell the group that these choices are arranged in no particular order and that you need their help in reordering or prioritizing the list, using the criteria. Start at the top of the list and follow the technique—each time asking the group which of the two pairs is best at meeting the criteria. When there are no more changes in the order of the list, debrief participants' reactions and discuss when to use or not use the tool.

DEBRIEFING

♦ Note that each tool has its strengths and weaknesses and that everyone must make his or her judgment about which tools will be most helpful in generating the best results in any situation.

♦ Explain that each tool can be used at various times in the PSDM process, but that care should be taken to use the tool for its intended purpose (for example, the Is/Is Not Matrix is good at narrowing a problem definition but is less effective at exploring the causes of the problem, although hints of cause can be uncovered using the tool).

◆ Point out that there are other tools that they should become familiar with when they have practiced and mastered these basic ones. Refer interested participants to other references (included in the For Further Reading section at the end of this book).

Learning Activity 11–30: Personal Action Planning

OBJECTIVE

The objective of this learning activity is to enable participants to select a specific problem with which they are dealing or a decision they need to make and to identify which tools from the Tool Kit they will use in addressing this problem or decision.

MATERIALS

◆ PowerPoint slide 10–17

◆ Training Instrument 11–24: Personal Plan for Using PSDM Tools

TIME

◆ 20 minutes

INSTRUCTIONS

1. Distribute Training Instrument 11–24 as you display slide 10–17. Emphasize the importance of translating the insights gained by practicing the tools in the PSDM Tool Kit into their daily practice.

2. Ask participants to work by themselves and identify one or two specific problems, issues, challenges, or decisions that they are facing at the present time.

3. Instruct them to identify which of the tools from the Tool Kit they will use and how they will use the tools to address their situation. Give them four or five minutes to work on their personal plans.

4. Invite participants to pair up and, for the next five minutes, share their specific situation(s) and the tools they plan to use to deal with the situation(s). Encourage each partner to offer additional insights and approaches for tackling the situation.

5. Reconvene the large group. As time permits, ask volunteers to share their situation(s) and describe the tools that they plan to use.

DEBRIEFING

◆ Emphasize the importance of making a commitment to use these tools beyond today's workshop.

◆ Encourage participants to continue revising their plans and trying out new tools to further address their issue.

Training Tools

- ◆ A workshop evaluation that elicits participants' reactions to your training program

- ◆ Five training tools to support and enhance the learning environment

This chapter describes training tools that support and enhance learning. Using any of these tools is optional, but we believe that effective trainers bring all the available resources to the workshop and they employ whatever materials, tools, and environmental arrangements they think will help their learners grasp, own, and put to use the concepts and practices they're sharing. Consider each of the tools in this chapter and decide for yourself how you can use them to make your training program more vital and more successful.

Tools 12–1 through 12–4 appear in .pdf format on the accompanying CD and can be printed from there.

Tool 12–1: Training Room Configuration and Layout

How the training room is arranged critically affects learning. The way you organize participant seating influences their focus during the session (that is, toward the trainer, toward fellow participants, or toward both) and helps set expectations for interaction or involvement. Figure 12–1 in the tool offers a training room configuration that we have found to be most conducive to learning. Figure 12–2 presents a room arrangement that works best when developing the Strategic Issues Map (chapter 8) and for applying the tools in the PSDM Tool Kit (chapter 10).

Tool 12–2: Goal-Setting Worksheet

Having participants set specific learning goals and objectives for your Strategic Planning Workshop is an essential step that focuses their energy and attention on achieving meaningful results. Research into both goal setting and the expectancy theory of motivation (Vroom, 1964; Porter, and Lawler, 1968) suggests that people will have greater commitment to achieving an outcome (in this case, mastering a learning objective) if they are involved in developing a specific goal for themselves. Furthermore, the expectancy theory tells us that motivation to achieve a goal is enhanced by a combination of three questions:

1. If I try to achieve a specific goal, will I be successful?

2. If I am successful in achieving the goal, what are the outcomes I am likely to receive?

3. How important are these outcomes?

This goal-setting worksheet increases the participant's motivation to learn by asking him or her to

1. define a specific personal goal

2. identify the likely rewards/outcomes to be realized by achieving that learning objective

3. describe the personal importance of these rewards/outcomes.

This activity helps target participants' attention to learning and therefore helps them increase the likelihood that they will realize a reward or outcome that they value highly.

Tool 12–3: Ah-Ha! Sheet

The Ah-Ha! Sheet is a simple tool to focus participants' learning. During the training day, participants are immersed in a wide variety of new ideas, models, methods, and strategies. Some of these ideas will stick easily and become part of the participants' new consciousness. Others, however—no matter how useful or relevant—can be lost as the learner integrates new knowledge and skills into practice.

If they use the Ah-Ha! Sheet to recognize and record in their own words the significant learning moments, ideas, methods, and strategies, they are more likely to retain their learning.

The Ah-Ha! Sheet also serves as an after-the-training memory jogger that reminds participants of key learning points from the session.

Tool 12–4: Workshop Level 1 Evaluation

Evaluating the effectiveness of your training program gives you an opportunity to measure the impact that the training has had on participant learning and behavior and on organizational results, and it offers you ideas for improving or enhancing the workshop for future sessions.

There are many variations of program design available, and we encourage you to review training evaluation literature and resources to develop your own or use what others have developed.

In his book *The Winning Trainer,* Julius Eitington (1996) offered a wide variety of training evaluation tools, with emphasis on those that actively involve participants. In the chapter titled "Using Participative Methods to Evaluate Training" he presented both quantitative methods (the reaction sheet) to group processes and post-training follow-up learning/behavior change assessments.

Two other useful resources are *ASTD Trainer's Tool Kit: Evaluation Instruments* (1991) and *ASTD Trainer's Tool Kit: More Evaluation Instruments* (1999). Both books offer a range of training evaluation forms used by organizations throughout the United States and include articles from *Training & Development.*

ASTD's "Learning Outcomes Report" (available for download by ASTD members in .pdf format in the research section of the ASTD Website) is published annually and highlights the results of efforts to measure organizational investments in education and training. The report includes multiple training evaluation forms (reaction sheets and follow-up assessments) that were used in the research and are available to the training community. Interested organizations can also participate in ASTD's ongoing research on this topic by becoming part of the annual study of learning outcomes.

Tool 12–5: The Parking Lot

In the course of many training workshops, issues and questions arise that neither the trainer nor participants are able to address or have time to tackle. The Parking Lot is a place to "park" ideas and questions for a future discussion. Also known as an Issues Bin or Future File, the Parking Lot can be useful in valuing a question or issue by recording it on a flipchart page. This Parking

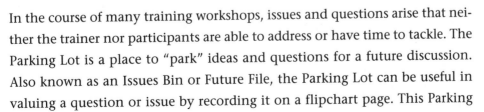

Lot for ideas and questions can then be revisited later in the training session, in a follow-up session (when answers have been gathered), or in communications with participants following the workshop.

The usefulness of the Parking Lot is in honoring the issues and questions participants bring to the session while not distracting the session with matters that either are off target for the session or cannot be addressed by the people in the room.

To create the Parking Lot simply post a blank flipchart page labeled *Parking Lot* where it is accessible to everyone at all times. This tool is particularly useful for strategic-planning workshops because it helps identify issues that *must* be addressed in an organization's strategic-planning efforts.

 ## Tool 12–6: Selecting Group Leaders

When you instruct participants to "discuss this in your small groups," it is useful to have each group select a discussion or group leader. Leaders focus the energy of the group and help create some accountability for the assigned task. It is also a good idea to encourage the rotation of leadership among the group members to distribute participation and responsibility.

Here are some ideas for selecting and rotating group leaders. Members might choose

- the person with the first or last birthday in the year, or the birthday closest to July 4th or to the current date

- the person with the most distinctive middle name

- the person who traveled the greatest or least distance from home to attend this workshop

- the person sitting to the right or the left of the previous discussion leader

- the most- or least-senior person in terms of years with the organization.

Using the Compact Disc

Insert the CD and locate the file *How to Use This CD.doc.*

Contents of the CD

The compact disc that accompanies this workbook on training in strategic planning and decision making contains three types of files. All of the files can be used on a variety of computer platforms.

- **Adobe .pdf documents.** These include handouts, tools, and training instruments.

- **Microsoft PowerPoint presentations.** These presentations add interest and depth to many of the training activities included in the workbook.

- **Microsoft PowerPoint files of overhead transparency masters.** These files makes it easy to print viewgraphs and handouts in black-and-white rather than using an office copier. They contain only text and line drawings; there are no images to print in grayscale.

Unlike other books in this series, *all* of the handouts, tools, and training instruments used in the strategic-planning training workshops appear *only* on this CD.

Computer Requirements

To read or print the .pdf files on the CD, you must have Adobe Acrobat Reader software installed on your system. The program can be downloaded free of cost from the Adobe Website, *www.adobe.com.*

To use or adapt the contents of the PowerPoint presentation files on the CD, you must have Microsoft PowerPoint software installed on your system. If you simply want to view the PowerPoint documents, you must have an appropriate viewer installed on your system. Microsoft provides various viewers free for downloading from its Website, *www.microsoft.com.*

Printing From the CD

TEXT FILES

You can print the training materials using Adobe Acrobat Reader. Simply open the .pdf file and print as many copies as you need. The following .pdf documents can be directly printed from the CD:

- Handout 11–1: Fallacies of Strategic Planning
- Handout 11–2: Characteristics of Enduring Organizations
- Handout 11–3: Strategic Planning Is . . .
- Handout 11–4: Strategic Thinking Is . . .
- Handout 11–5: Strategic Thinking, Strategy Formulation, and Implementation
- Handout 11–6: Developing Strategic Thinkers
- Handout 11–7: Strategies for Escaping from the Tactical
- Handout 11–8: An Integrated Strategic-Planning Model
- Handout 11–9: Actions for Each Strategic-Planning Stage
- Handout 11–10: Common Obstacles to Developing and Implementing a Strategic Plan
- Handout 11–11: The Role and Power of an Organization's Shared Vision
- Handout 11–12: Characteristics of an Inspiring Vision
- Handout 11–13: Sample Vision Statements
- Handout 11–14: Characteristics of Core Values
- Handout 11–15: Sample Core Values
- Handout 11–16: The SWOT Analysis: Understanding the Organization's Environment
- Handout 11–17: Selecting the Strategic Agenda
- Handout 11–18: Template for Strategic Action Planning
- Handout 11–19: Sample Strategic Action Plan
- Handout 11–20: Lessons from Chaos and Complexity Theories
- Handout 11–21: Exploring the Strategic Issues Map
- Handout 11–22: Seven "Breakthrough Thinking" Principles to Guide Strategic PSDM
- Handout 11–23: A Model for Problem Solving
- Handout 11–24: Writing Clear Problem Statements

◆ Handout 11–25: A Model for Strategic Decision Making

◆ Handout 11–26: The Decision Matrix

◆ Handout 11–27: When to Involve or Not Involve Others

◆ Handout 11–28: Strategic PSDM Tool Kit

◆ Tool 12–1, Figure 1: Optimal Training Room Arrangement

◆ Tool 12–1, Figure 2: Optimal Training Room Arrangement When Using a Wallchart

◆ Tool 12–2: Goal-Setting Worksheet

◆ Tool 12–3: Ah-Ha! Sheet

◆ Tool 12–4: Workshop Level 1 Evaluation

◆ Training Instrument 11–1: Ensuring Organizational Success

◆ Training Instrument 11–2: Perceptions of Strategic Planning

◆ Training Instrument 11–3: Why Should We Have a Strategic Plan?

◆ Training Instrument 11–4: Purpose and Goals of Strategic Planning

◆ Training Instrument 11–5: Actions to Develop Strategic Thinkers

◆ Training Instrument 11–6: Personal Plan for Strategic Thinking

◆ Training Instrument 11–7: Levels of Planning in Organizations

◆ Training Instrument 11–8: Stages of the Strategic Plan Development Process

◆ Training Instrument 11–9: Who Develops the Strategic Plan?

◆ Training Instrument 11–10: Personal Plan for Strategic Involvement

◆ Training Instrument 11–11: Organizational Strengths to Support and Sustain the Strategic Plan

◆ Training Instrument 11–12: Actions to Address Potential Obstacles

◆ Training Instrument 11–13: Discovering Core Values

◆ Training Instrument 11–14: Personal Action Plan for the Lessons from Chaos

◆ Training Instrument 11–15: Implications and Actions from the Strategic Issues Map

◆ Training Instrument 11–16: Personal Planning for Strategic Thinking from the Strategic Issues Map

◆ Training Instrument 11–17: Definitions of a Problem and a Decision

◆ Training Instrument 11–18: Exploring Your Problem-Solving and Decision-Making History

- Training Instrument 11–19: Approaches to Problem Solving and Decision Making
- Training Instrument 11–20: Your Imagination Quotient
- Training Instrument 11–21: What's the Problem?
- Training Instrument 11–22: Decision Matrix Application
- Training Instrument 11–23: When to Involve Others
- Training Instrument 11–24: Personal Plan for Problem-Solving and Decision-Making Tools

POWERPOINT SLIDES

You can print the presentation slides directly from this CD using Microsoft PowerPoint. Simply open the .ppt files and print as many copies as you need. You can also make handouts of the presentations by printing two, four, or six slides per page. These slides will be in color, with design elements embedded. PowerPoint also permits you to print these in grayscale or black-and-white, although printing from the overhead masters file will yield better black-and-white representations. Many trainers who use personal computers to project their presentations bring along viewgraphs just in case there are glitches in the system. The overhead masters can be printed from the PowerPoint .pps files.

Adapting the PowerPoint Slides

You can modify or otherwise customize the slides by opening and editing them in the appropriate application. However, you must retain the denotation of the original source of the material—it is illegal to pass it off as your own work. You may indicate that a document was adapted from this workbook, copyrighted by ASTD, Jeff Russell, and Linda Russell. The files will open as Read Only, "so before you adapt them you will need to save them onto your hard drive under a different file name.

Showing the PowerPoint Presentations

On the CD, the following PowerPoint presentations are included:

- Fundamentals.ppt
- Advanced Issues.ppt
- Strategic Thinkers.ppt
- Strategic PSDM.ppt
- Tools.ppt

Table A–1
Navigating Through a PowerPoint Presentation

KEY	POWERPOINT "SHOW" ACTION
Space bar *or* Enter *or* Mouse click	Advance through custom animations embedded in the presentation
Backspace	Back up to the last projected element of the presentation
Escape	Abort the presentation
B *or* b	Blank the screen to black
B *or* b *(repeat)*	Resume the presentation
W *or* w	Blank the screen to white
W *or* w *(repeat)*	Resume the presentation

Having the presentations in .ppt format means that they automatically show full-screen when you double-click on a file name. You also can open Microsoft PowerPoint and launch the presentations from there.

Use the space bar, the enter key, or mouse clicks to advance through a show. Press the backspace key to back up. Use the escape key to abort a presentation. If you want to blank the screen to black while the group discusses a point, press the B key. Pressing it again restores the show. If you want to blank the screen to a white background, do the same with the W key. Table A–1 summarizes these instructions.

We strongly recommend that trainers practice making presentations with the PowerPoint slides before using them in live training situations. You should be confident that you can cogently expand on the points featured in the presentations and discuss the methods for working through them. If you want to engage your training participants fully (rather than worrying about how to show the next slide), become familiar with this simple technology *before* you need to use it. A good practice is to insert notes into the *Speaker's Notes* feature of the PowerPoint program, print them out, and have them in front of you when you present the slides.

For Further Reading

ADULT LEARNING AND TRAINING PROGRAM DESIGN/EVALUATION

ASTD. *ASTD Trainer's Toolkit: Evaluation Instruments.* Alexandria, VA: ASTD Press, 1991.

————. *ASTD Trainer's Toolkit: More Evaluation Instruments.* Alexandria, VA: ASTD Press, 1999.

Broad, Mary, and John Newstrom. *Transfer of Training.* Reading, MA: Addison-Wesley, 1992.

Brookfield, Stephen D. *Understanding and Facilitating Adult Learning.* San Francisco: Jossey-Bass, 1991.

Eitington, Julius E. *The Winning Trainer* (3rd edition). Houston, TX: Gulf Publishing, 1996.

Kirkpatrick, D. L. *Evaluating Training Programs: The Four Levels* (2nd edition). San Francisco: Berrett-Koehler, 1994.

Phillips. Jack L. *Return on Investment in Training and Performance Improvement Programs: A Step-By-Step Manual for Calculating the Financial Return on Investment* (2nd edition). Burlington, MA: Butterworth-Heinemann, Gulf Professional Publishing, 2003.

Renner, Peter Franz. *The Instructor's Survival Kit: A Handbook for Teachers and Adults* (2nd edition). Vancouver, BC: Training Associates, 1989.

Russell, Lou. *The Accelerated Learning Fieldbook.* San Francisco: Jossey-Bass/Pfeiffer, 1999.

STRATEGIC PLANNING AND PROBLEM SOLVING

Allison, G. T. *Essence of Decision.* Boston: Little, Brown, 1971.

Andrews, Kenneth. *The Concept of Corporate Strategy.* Homewood, IL: Irwin-Dorsey Press, 1987.

Ansoff, H. Igor. *Corporate Strategy.* New York: McGraw-Hill, 1965.

Argyris, Chris, and Donald Schon. *Organizational Learning.* Reading, MA: Addison-Wesley, 1978.

Boyd, B. K. Strategic Planning and Financial Performance: A Meta-Analytical Review. *Journal of Management Studies* July 1991: 353–74.

Brown, Shona, and Kathleen Eisenhardt. *Competing on the Edge: Strategy as Structured Chaos.* Boston: Harvard Business School Press, 1998.

Collins, James. *Good to Great: Why Some Companies Make the Leap and Others Don't.* New York: HarperCollins, 2001.

Collins, James, and Jerry Porras. *Built to Last: Successful Habits of Visionary Companies.* New York: HarperBusiness, HarperCollins, 1994.

Cooperrider, David L., Diana Whitney, and Jacqueline Stavros. *Appreciative Inquiry Handbook: The First in a Series of AI Workbooks for Leaders of Change.* Bedford Heights, OH: Lakeshore Publishers, 2003.

de Geus, Arie. *The Living Company.* Boston: Harvard Business School Press, 1997.

Hamel, Gary, and C. K. Prahalad. *Competing for the Future.* Boston: Harvard Business School Press, 1994.

Hannan and J. Freeman. The Population Ecology of Organizations. *American Journal of Sociology* 82 (5): 929–64.

Kaplan, Robert S., and David Norton. *The Balanced Scorecard.* Boston: Harvard Business School Press, 1996.

Klein, Gary. *Sources of Power: How People Make Decisions.* Cambridge, MA: MIT Press, 1998.

Michalko, Michael. *ThinkerToys: A Handbook of Business Creativity for the 90s.* Berkeley, CA: Ten Speed Press, 1991.

Miles, R., and C. Snow. *Organizational Strategy, Structure, and Process.* New York: McGraw-Hill, 1978.

Mintzberg, H. Patterns in Strategy Formation. *Management Science* 24 (9): 934–48.

————. *The Rise and Fall of Strategic Planning.* New York: Free Press, 1994.

Mintzberg, Henry, Bruce Ahlstrand, and Joseph Lampel. *Strategy Safari: A Guided Tour through the Wilds of Strategic Management.* New York: Free Press, 1998.

Nadler, Gerald, and Shozo Hibino. *Breakthrough Thinking.* Rocklin, CA: Prima Publishing, 1990.

Nohria, Nitin, William Joyce, and Bruce Roberson. What Really Works. *Harvard Business Review* July 2003: 43–52.

Norman, Richard. *Management for Growth.* New York: John Wiley & Sons, 1977.

Pfeffer, Jeffrey. *Competitive Advantage through People: Unleashing the Power of the Work Force.* Boston: Harvard Business School Press, 1994.

Pfeffer, J., and G. Salancik. *The External Control of Organizations.* New York: Harper & Row, 1978.

Porter, Michael. *Competitive Strategy.* New York: Free Press, 1980.

Rhenman, Eric. *Organization Theory for Long Range Planning.* London: John Wiley, 1973.

Sanders, T. Irene. *Strategic Thinking and the New Science: Planning in the Midst of Chaos, Complexity, and Change.* New York: Free Press, 1998.

Schwartz, Peter. *The Art of the Long View.* New York: Doubleday Currency, 1991.

Senge, Peter M. *The Fifth Discipline.* New York: Doubleday Currency, 1990.

Simon, Herbert. *The New Science of Management Decisions.* New York: Prentice Hall, 1977.

Stacey, Ralph D. *Managing the Unknowable.* San Francisco: Jossey-Bass, 1992.

———. *Strategic Management and Organisational Dynamics.* London: Prentice Hall/Financial Times, 2003.

Stacey, Ralph D., Douglas Griffin, and Patricia Shaw. *Complexity and Management.* London: Routledge, 2002.

Stern, C. W., and G. Stalk (eds.). *Perspectives on Strategy.* New York: John Wiley & Sons, 1998.

Weisbord, Marvin. *Discovering Common Ground.* San Francisco: Berrett-Koehler, 1992.

Weisbord, Marvin, and Sandra Janoff. *Future Search.* San Francisco: Berrett-Koehler, 1995

Wheatley, Margaret J. *Leadership and the New Science.* San Francisco: Berrett-Koehler, 1992, 1994.

EXPECTANCY THEORY OF MOTIVATION

Porter, L. W., and E. E. Lawler. *Managerial Attitudes and Performance.* Homewood, Ill: Irwin-Dorsey, 1968.

Vroom, V. H. *Work and Motivation.* New York: John Wiley & Sons, 1964.

Jeffrey and Linda Russell are the founders and co-directors of Russell Consulting, Inc., headquartered in Madison, Wisconsin. For almost 20 years Jeff and Linda have provided consulting and training services in such areas as leadership, strategic thinking and planning, leading change, employee quality of work life surveys, organizational development, performance coaching, and performance management. Their diverse list of clients includes *Fortune* 500 companies, small businesses, social or nonprofit organizations, and government agencies.

Jeff has a bachelor of arts degree in humanism and cultural change and a master of arts degree in industrial relations, both from the University of Wisconsin. He serves as an adjunct faculty member for that university, teaching for the Small Business Development Center, the Wisconsin Certified Public Manager Program, and a number of other certification programs with the University of Wisconsin campuses. He is a frequent presenter at local, state, regional, and international conferences.

Linda has a bachelor of arts degree in social work and completed graduate work in rehabilitation counseling. She specializes in designing and implementing quality of work life surveys and in facilitating team and organizational development interventions.

Jeff and Linda have authored four previous books, including *Leading Change Training* (ASTD Press, 2003), and they publish *Workplace Enhancement Notes,* a journal of tips for leading organizations.

With a company vision of helping create and sustain great organizations, Russell Consulting, Inc., integrates theory, research, and real-world experience in its daily consulting and training practice. Jeff and Linda help their clients find practical management solutions to a challenging world that too often offers strategies that are long on hype and short on substance.

Readers wanting to know more about Jeff and Linda and their work are encouraged to visit www.RussellConsultingInc.com or to send them an email at RCI@RussellConsultingInc.com. Please contact them if you have questions about the ideas in this book or would be interested in arranging for RCI's consulting or training services.